Star Quarterbacks of the NFL

In this book Bill Libby tells the stories of ten quarterbacks who dominate the NFL—how they overcame difficulties, developed their talents and skills, and finally helped lead their teams to victory. The players included are Roman Gabriel, Greg Cook, Bob Griese, Sonny Jurgensen, Joe Namath, Craig Morton, Bill Nelsen, Joe Kapp, Daryle Lamonica and Lenny Dawson.

Star Quarterbacks of the NFL

by Bill Libby

Illustrated with photographs

RANDOM HOUSE · NEW YORK

For Allyson

Photograph Credits: Vernon J. Biever: 9, 75, 115, 122–123, 129, 142, 162; Chance Brockway: 27; Malcolm Emmons: front and back endpaper, title page, vii, 2, 12, 15, 20, 44, 50, 51, 54, 61, 64–65, 67, 70, 80–81, 95, 104, 110–111, 113, 118, 132, 136, 146, 151, 154, 166, 170; Emmons and Brockway: 36; Fred Kaplan: 84; United Press International: 30–31, 88, 98, 101.

Cover photo (Daryle Lamonica): Ken Regan

Contents

Introduction

The *Star Quarterbacks of the NFL* include many to whom success came slowly. Joe Namath and Bill Nelsen could not make the grade when they first began their high school careers; Greg Cook and Lenny Dawson were only ordinary performers.

Sonny Jurgensen and Daryle Lamonica were not outstanding in college competition. The college teams of Cook and Craig Morton won less than half their games during their varsity careers. Lamonica was passed over by the pro teams several times before he was drafted late. Interest in Joe Kapp was so slight that he decided to play pro ball in Canada instead.

Many of the star quarterbacks played very little in their early years as professionals. Lamonica had to be traded from one team to another before he got his chance to become a star. Dawson had to wait five years and endure two trades.

Nevertheless, all have become great quarterbacks. Today they dominate the National Football League, taking the places of Johnny Unitas, Bart Starr and others, who were profiled in an earlier Punt, Pass and Kick Library book, *Great Quarterbacks of the NFL*.

The quarterback is the single most important and most glamorous performer in football and the star quarterbacks seldom attain that stardom without struggle and pain. Each has a different story to tell and the stories of ten top performers who have risen to rare prominence are told on the following pages.

1

Roman Gabriel

*Gabriel calls signals in the crucial game
against Baltimore.*

In the final game of the National Football
League's regular 1967 season, more than 75,000 persons packed the sprawling Coliseum in Los Angeles
on a warm winter afternoon. Millions more
throughout the country watched on their television
sets. The Baltimore Colts were playing the Rams
and the winner would be the Coastal Division
champion. The stakes were high and the fans were
roaring.

Johnny Unitas, perhaps the greatest quarterback
in football history, led the Colts to an early 7-3 lead
and was driving them toward another score when
the Colt march stalled. The Colts tried a field goal,
which missed. The Rams took over on their 20-yard
line and on the next play Roman Gabriel threw
deep to flanker Jack Snow. Snow caught the ball and
ran into the end zone to complete an 80-yard scoring
pass. The Rams jumped into the lead as their fans
screamed with delight.

That single play seemed to switch the momentum

from the Colts to the Rams. The old pro, Unitas, drove the Colts back downfield. But "The Fearsome Foursome," the Rams' famed defensive line, applied pressure to Unitas until he bent, throwing the ball badly as he was hit. The Rams intercepted with time running out in the first half. Gabriel marched the Rams 81 yards to score again, completing the drive with a pass to Bernie Casey with 10 seconds left in the half. The Rams led, 17-7.

The favored Baltimore team came back in the second half, determined to assert its superiority. Unitas led his mates to a field goal that cut the difference to seven points. Then he mounted another drive to try to tie the score. However, he was hit while throwing. He buckled, and his toss went soft. Jack Pardee intercepted the ball, turning it back to Gabriel's offensive unit.

The Rams rolled deep into Colt territory. They had reached the Baltimore 37 when Gabriel faded back to pass. The Colts were blitzing and Gabriel was hit as hard as Unitas had been hit by the Rams a few minutes earlier. However, "Gabe" is younger and bigger than "Johnny U." Roman braced as the tackler bounced off him, tearing away part of his uniform. Roman got the pass off to Bernie Casey, who made the catch for a first down. A few moments later, Gabriel threw to tight end Bill Truax in the end zone and the Rams had the game wrapped up.

The king of the quarterbacks had been dethroned. The small, though skilled, Unitas contin-

4

ued to play, and he was still brilliant, but in his middle 30s he was no longer the performer he once had been. Gabriel, on the other hand, had matured in his late 20s to become the most consistently outstanding quarterback in the game. At a height of 6-foot-3 and weight of 225 pounds, the powerful Roman became the model for the new breed of quarterbacks in the violent world of pro football.

As Gabriel ran off the field that day, the cheers of the great crowd poured out from all parts of the great stadium. He had attained his peak after years of struggling to master perhaps the most demanding position in sports. Two years later, in 1969, he would be named Most Valuable Player in the league.

Roman Gabriel's father left the Philippines in 1925. He worked as a laborer in Alaska and California before settling in Wilmington, North Carolina, where he worked in railroad dining cars. Roman was born on August 5, 1940. He has been called, "the world's biggest Filipino." However, he laughingly suggests that he inherited his size as much from his mother, a hearty woman of Irish stock, as from his 6-foot father. Until he reached his teens, the younger Gabriel was actually small for his age. He was also sickly, suffering from asthma, an affliction which disappeared in later years.

Roman was an only child throughout most of his early life. (Another son was born to the Gabriels when Roman was 12.) Roman's father encouraged him in sports and hung a basket on a wall bordering their tiny backyard almost as soon as the boy began to walk. However, the older Gabriel was strict with the boy. Roman recalls an incident that occurred when he was five years old. His father called him for supper and Roman said he would be in when he was through playing. The father, who had been shaving, laid down his razor, picked up his old-fashioned razor strap, and took off after his son. "He caught me and beat me," Roman remembers. "I never was a problem after that."

Roman describes himself as a "stubborn kid." As a boy, his asthma was so severe he could not walk the several blocks to grade school without having to stop to sit on a curb to catch his breath. However, the asthma gradually disappeared. He stuck to sports until his skill more than balanced his lack of size and strength. He remembers one day when he tried out as a catcher for Little League baseball.

"On the first pitch, the batter started to swing and I flinched," he recalls. "I turned my head and the ball hit the side of my jaw. I never flinched again."

By the time he reached New Hanover High School in Wilmington, North Carolina, Roman was growing tall and beginning to fill out. Although he was a fine all-around athlete who was considered a pro baseball and basketball prospect, football was his best game. He wishfully aspired to follow in the footsteps of a former New Hanover High star, Sonny Jurgensen, who had gone on to Duke and the NFL. A poor boy, Roman would not ordinarily have attended college, but some 50 schools offered the young passer athletic scholarships.

Roman attended North Carolina State, where he earned All-America honors. Although surrounded by a mediocre team, he completed 286 of 506 passes for 2,951 yards and 19 touchdowns in three years. Meanwhile the pro scouts had studied his every move. It was clear that he was big enough and strong enough to make the NFL. He seemed smart enough and determined enough, too. But there were those who wondered if the Carolina quarterback was quick enough, and some even wondered if he was stable enough.

Gabriel was a shy, sensitive young man. In college, he had gone his own way until he was considered almost a recluse. He had become so lonely during his sophomore year that he had talked his high school sweetheart, Suzanne Horton, into quitting nearby East Carolina College in order to marry him. He felt he needed someone who understood his moody ways.

He was uncomfortable with fame. When his own fans chanted, "Throw, Gabriel, throw!" (a take-off on "Blow, Gabriel, blow!"), he hung his head. When writers or fans sought to talk to him, he hid. When a newspaper photographer invaded a classroom to snap his picture, Gabriel threw him out. Still, the Los Angeles Rams selected him on the first round of the NFL draft of graduating college seniors.

When Roman joined the team in 1962, the Rams had won only ten games during the preceeding three seasons. Bob Waterfield was the coach. Waterfield had been a great pro quarterback himself, and Gabriel assumed the coach would give him special attention. Waterfield, however, was an unusually quiet and moody man, too. He did not give much of himself to any of his players. Thus the Rams went with a veteran quarterback, Zeke Bratkowski. Waterfield was fired after winning only one of the first eight games in 1962, and Harland Svare took over as coach. Svare stayed with Bratkowski, but failed to win a game during the remainder of the campaign. Gabriel appeared in only six games all season.

In 1963, Svare went with either Bratkowski or Terry Baker (a Heisman Trophy winner) in the first five games. But with an 0-5 record and a bunch of restless fans, Svare turned to Gabriel. Roman led the team to victories in five of the last nine outings.

Gabriel appeared to have made a place for himself as a regular. But when he was injured in the last exhibition game prior to the 1964 season, Svare turned to rookie Bill Munson and stayed with him the rest of the way. Gabriel played in only seven games. At

---

Roman takes the snap from center and begins his pivot.

the end of the season, Roman asked Svare to give him a regular role so he could prove or disprove his ability. Svare said he could give no guarantees.

In 1965, Svare again went with Munson. The team had won only one game when Munson suffered a broken leg. Gabriel took over and led the Rams to victories in three of their last four games. But by then he was disenchanted with the Rams and pro football.

In 1966, Al Davis, then the commissioner of the rival American Football League, instigated a series of raids on NFL rosters. The AFL was especially seeking star quarterbacks. Gabriel signed with the Oakland Raiders for four years at $100,000 a year. Soon after, however, Svare was fired and George Allen became the new coach of the Rams. One of his first moves was to promise Gabriel that he could be his regular quarterback if he stayed in Los Angeles. Gabriel already felt guilty about deserting his team-mates and signed a new contract with the Rams. But as it turned out his contract with Oakland was nullified anyway, because the two leagues merged.

When Allen took over as coach of the Rams, the team had some good talent though they were very disorganized. Allen traded away future draft choices and erratic young prospects for stable, proven veterans. Rapidly he rebuilt the Rams to respectability. With Gabriel in command, the team won eight of fourteen games in 1966. For the first time in nine seasons, they won more games than they lost. Still,

Gabriel brooded about how hastily he had signed his Ram contract and how the merger had removed from him any opportunity to fulfill the fatter offer from the Raiders. He decided to file a $200,000 lawsuit against the Rams and the NFL, an act for which he was generally criticized. Finally, in the interest of team harmony, he dropped the suit on the eve of the new 1967 season.

In 1967, Gabriel and the Rams compiled an 11-1-2 record, including the climactic conquest of the Colts that brought them the Coastal Division title, though they went on to lose to Green Bay in the Western Conference play-offs.

In 1968, Gabriel was one of many Rams to suffer injuries. The team slipped slightly to a 10-3-1 record and second place in their division. However, in 1969, the Rams and Gabriel bounced back to win their first eleven games, clinching divisional honors well before the season ended. Although they were nosed out by Minnesota in the conference play-offs, Gabriel had established himself as the All-Star quarterback and the league's MVP. Although his team was not quite yet at the top he, personally, had scaled the heights.

During the last four seasons of the 1960s, Gabriel completed more than 800 passes for more than 10,000 yards and 78 touchdowns. In eight seasons as a pro, he had completed more than 1,100 passes for more than 15,000 yards and 109 touchdowns. His accuracy was outstanding, and his interception rate

was so low that he was running ahead of the lifetime record for NFL passers. Most important, his leadership was unsurpassed. With Roman starting, the Rams had won on an average of eight out of every ten games.

"There was never any question in my mind that I could do the job as an NFL quarterback," Gabriel said after his 1969 banner year. "There *was* a question as to whether I'd ever get a real chance. Some promising players never do. They say it takes six or seven years to develop a top pro quarterback. I say it takes as long as it takes for you to play regularly for a while. After four seasons in this league, I was still as inexperienced as a rookie. Once I got my chance, I had to learn my job, but at least then I could progress rapidly."

Gabriel admits that his seasons of inactivity depressed him deeply. "Through high school and college ball, I was not only a starter but a star," he explained. "Suddenly, in pro ball, I was on the bench, a forgotten man. It hurt my love of the game, my dedication and my confidence. In one game early in my career, Svare even used me as a defensive end. That almost destroyed me. When I did play quarterback, he never let me call signals. He sent in the plays. I was nicknamed 'Roman the Robot,' which hurt my pride."

Gabriel passes against the Vikings as defensive end Carl Eller (81) rushes. The Rams lost the Playoff game, 23-20.

13

Therefore, Gabriel was ready to jump the Rams and, later, to sue them. "I felt I had been treated badly," he said. "We all have to grow up. During this ordeal, I matured. I still want to make the most money for myself and my family, but I see now the team must come first. If the team succeeds, we'll all do well. Svare simply did not think I was his best quarterback. I was fortunate that a man—Allen—came along who did. He let me call the plays, which gave me a reason to study the science of the game and the chance to perfect my profession and gain the confidence of my teammates."

Allen has as many nice things to say about his star quarterback. "Roman is intelligent and strong," he says. "He has a great throwing arm and powerful legs. He is durable. He plays with considerable confidence now and has the confidence of his teammates. He is the leader of this team and has become the best quarterback in football." All-Pro Ram defensive tackle Merlin Olsen adds, "If the players do not have faith in a play or a key player, they will not perform with that little extra snap that makes everything work. One day we looked at Gabe in the huddle and knew he could lead us to the top. Almost everything has worked from that day on."

Roman Gabriel's greatest strength *is* his physical strength. He is a giant among quarterbacks who

---

In danger of being tackled, Roman looks for running room.

seems able to throw a football the length of the field. He can flick it 50 yards with tacklers hitting him or hanging onto him. While the secret to success in pro football nowadays seems to be to "get the quarterback," even those who get to Gabriel have trouble bringing him down. Though not a scrambler, he is a rugged runner. He has endured several severe injuries. He overcame the knee injury which required an operation in 1966. He played the last part of 1968 with two broken bones in his throwing hand. During that same season he was hit from behind, knocked cold and, as a result, he missed ten minutes of the 17-16 upset loss to Chicago. That game removed the Rams from contention. He played the last part of 1969 with an extremely sore leg.

"I think the players in pro football are getting so big and fast these days that it takes a big quarterback to stand up to the pounding," Gabriel comments. "Also it helps enormously to have height that helps you to see above the linemen who come charging at you. It is easy to see open men if you're sitting in the stands. But difficult to see them in a maze of giants on the field."

Some say that the games are actually won during the week; they are only played on Sundays. Gabriel practices with his teammates six days a week. He is the first man on the field most days, and the last to leave it. He studies films with his teammates during most practice days, then takes films home for two hours or more of viewing at night. As the quarterback, he also has special conferences with the coaches to prepare the game plan each week. He must know every man's assignment on every one of 100 running and 150 passing plays. About 40 plays are selected for each game. Gabe is a demanding leader who once deliberately hit a teammate on the helmet with a pass because he felt he was loafing.

Gabriel and Allen have been criticized for being too conservative, especially in clutch games. The coach and quarterback agree on the system which calls for running as much as passing, and passing to the backs as well as to the ends, and they do grow cautious under pressure. "I am not a spectacular quarterback, so I may never be recognized as a great quarterback," Roman said. "But I believe I am the best quarterback in the game today. I do more things well than most. The only personal goal I think about is to be a complete quarterback."

For being the best quarterback in the game, or close to it, Roman earns an estimated $75,000 a season. There is additional money coming in, too, from a travel agency, a vitamin company, and a Volkswagen dealership. Gabriel himself drives a $7,000 Porsche, which is in keeping with his expensive tastes. He, his wife and their three sons live in a ten-room house with a huge yard and swimming pool in Long Beach, California.

Success has wiped out many of his shy, moody traits of the past. But with the Rams winning regularly, Roman is forced to dodge many of his admir-

17

ers, or he could spend the whole day signing his autograph. He has even discontinued going to basketball and baseball games in Los Angeles because the fans will not leave him alone to enjoy the games.

Gabriel knows that cheers can turn to boos rather quickly. And he knows that despite his success and the fact that the Rams seem so overpowering with him in the lineup, he has yet to play in a championship team. There are critics who believe that, if a star doesn't play for a title winner, he can scarcely be classified with the immortals—Baugh, Luckman, Graham, Unitas. Gabriel probably had this in mind, too, when he spoke after the 1970 Pro Bowl game. "It is all very nice—victories like this, individual laurels," he said while being congratulated for a late touchdown pass that triggered the West all-star team's 16-13 triumph. "But until my team wins the championship, I can't be satisfied. I'm glad to have gotten to the top. But what got me there was the desire to do more than the next fellow, and there remains much more to be done."

2
Greg Cook

Greg Cook drops back to pass during his rookie season with the Bengals.

During an exhibition game between the New York Jets and the Philadelphia Eagles in 1968, Greg Cook was chased from behind the Jet bench by a Cincinnati policeman and hustled toward a patrol car. Fortunately for Cook, Coach Ray Callahan of the University of Cincinnati rushed up to explain that the protesting young man in the officer's grasp was his quarterback. The young Cincinnati player had merely been trying to get a closer look at the Jets' fabled Joe Namath. Callahan pleaded for mercy, which was granted.

Later, Callahan and Cook proceeded to the Jets' locker room. Callahan, it turned out, had arranged in advance for post-game passes as well as an introduction to Namath.

Greg met Namath; he came away unimpressed.

"He was rude," said Greg. "He acted like we were wasting his time."

After that cold reception, Greg Cook determined he was going to surpass Namath in the pros. He got

21

off to a spectacular start. As a rookie professional in 1969, Cook performed much better than Namath had in his first year. In fact, on the basis of Cook's first-year performance, many observers felt Cook just might surpass Namath in years to come.

At a height of 6 feet, 4 inches and weight of 220 pounds, Greg Cook is cut from the mold that Roman Gabriel has made fashionable for quarterback stars. Much more handsome than Namath, with blond hair swirling mod-style about his face, Greg says, "There's a hairline difference between confidence and overconfidence and I'm sitting right on that line."

If he succeeds, it will be a classic case of a young man resisting early discouragement, maturing late and surging suddenly to become a super star.

Gregory Lynn Cook was born November 20, 1946, in Chillicothe, Ohio. His father was a physical-fitness instructor at a state correctional institution for the criminally insane. But the Cook family lived apart from this depressing atmosphere. The father had played one year of professional baseball in his youth, and encouraged his four sons to participate in sports.

For a while Greg appeared an unlikely candidate to make a career of sports. He played baseball and basketball, as well as football, at Chillicothe High School. But at first he was skinny, awkward and far from outstanding. During his four seasons of high school football, he played for four different coaches. This made it impossible to learn any one system. By his final season, however, Greg was physically big enough and strong enough to interest the University of Cincinnati in his quarterbacking potential. Since none of the Big Ten schools seemed enthusiastic about him, he was satisfied to settle for a less demanding circuit in which his foes included such teams as Xavier, Tampa and Tulsa.

During his sophomore year, Cook broke a bone in his throwing hand so he saw service in only six games, passing for 413 yards. Then a new coach arrived on the scene, and Greg had to adjust to still another playing system. As a junior, however, he progressed rapidly, passing for 1,221 yards. And as a senior he really hit his stride, ranking first in the nation with 3,272 yards and 25 touchdown passes.

At the University the rangy thrower had exceptional receivers, but scant support otherwise. The Cincinnati Bearcats won only eleven games during his three seasons. Without adequate defense, they were sometimes outscored no matter how many points Cook put on the scoreboard. For example, he passed for 352 yards and three touchdowns against the University of Houston but was beaten, 71-33! He tossed for 264 yards and four touchdowns against Tulsa, but was defeated, 55-34. He threw for an NCAA record—554 yards and four touchdowns—against Ohio U. and was beaten, 60-48!

Gritty Greg kept pitching, however. During his

senior year he participated in touchdown plays that measured 53, 53, 66, 68, 69, 74, 85 and 95 yards. He could pick apart a defense and would free a receiver for a short pass or, if necessary, throw the length of the field to a fast-stepping teammate. Big, solid and powerful, Greg could make plays under dreadful defensive pressure. Once, as he was being hit by a Texas Tech tackler who had a hand on his face, he threw a pass that produced a 53-yard touchdown and a 10-10 tie.

Greg set a school record by passing for 396 yards in a 37-7 lashing of Louisville. He surpassed this with a record 554 yards achieved during a game the Bearcats finally lost to Ohio University, 60-48. In the same game he completed 35 of 56 passes. Was he recklessly putting the ball in the air? Definitely not! He was intercepted on his first throw, then not again.

In his college finale at Cincinnati's Nippert Stadium, Cook fired for 407 yards, rallying the Bearcats to a 23-21 conquest of arch-rival Miami of Ohio. He threw for three late touchdowns, dramatically settling the issue by completing 18 of 22 passes, in an awesome fourth-quarter surge. Nine of those completions were consecutive.

After the game, Cook stripped off his soggy Cincinnati uniform for the last time and awaited his professional fate. Although he was denied All-America status, he had been singled out as a prime prospect for the pro teams. O. J. Simpson went first in the draft, followed by George Kunz, Leroy Keyes and Joe Greene. Cook went fifth—to the Cincinnati Bengals, who played their home games in Nippert Stadium, his collegiate playing field. Some observers suspected that hometown sentiment had influenced the Bengals to pick an untested youngster, but Cook quickly proved that coach Paul Brown had been the shrewdest of the selectors.

In the college All-Star Game at Soldier Field in Chicago, Cook met Joe Namath head on. The College All-Stars were facing Namath's Jets, fresh from their resounding Super Bowl victory. In recent years, the pros had been mauling the collegians to such an extent that sportswriters expected the annual classic to be discontinued. Cook may have saved the game. After the All-Stars had fallen far behind with Notre Dame's All-America Terry Hanratty at quarterback, All-Star coach Otto Graham summoned Cook. Greg connected on 12 of 23 passes for 241 yards and three touchdowns. The pros had to scramble to salvage a 26-24 win.

The performance proved that Cook was ready for the pros without the usual years of apprenticeship. Fortunately for him, he had joined an expansion team which was willing to let him play while he learned.

Although the Bengals were a weak team, Cook made them dangerous. After gaining experience on the exhibition trail, Greg made a spectacular debut by completing 11 of 21 passes for 155 yards. This included touchdown tosses of 25 and 69 yards to Eric Crabtree, to pace a 27-21 conquest of the visiting Miami Dolphins.

Since Miami was also an expansion team, most experts remained unconvinced. Then the San Diego Chargers, a strong veteran team, arrived for the second game of the season. Cook proceeded to cut down the Chargers, too, hurling 14 completions in 22 passes for 327 yards and a 34-20 upset. He passed 9 yards for one score, 39 for another, 78 for a third, and ran 9 for a fourth. He was as spry as a kid, yet poised as a veteran. The cheers echoed through the stadium and the press called him "Superman" and "Golden Boy."

Coach Brown, the controversial coach who had made the NFL Cleveland Browns the dominant team of the 1950s before he moved on to Cincinnati, called Cook the best quarterback prospect he had seen since the days of Otto Graham, Brown's field general in Cleveland. "There will be ups and downs —some downs Greg doesn't even know about yet," Brown cautioned, "but he has the stuff of greatness. Our future is tied to him. I'm guarding him like a mother hen."

As mother hen, Brown shuttled players from the sidelines, calling all offensive signals for Cook as he had done in the past with Graham. Graham had

Finding no receiver upfield, Greg decides to run with the ball.

26

come to resent it, and many said the Bengals would be stifled by Brown's methods. But Cook insisted his coach was helpful. "I'm studying the pro game and learning," he said. "In the meantime I don't have to be concerned with plotting strategy, only executing it. The record book shows Brown's way won for Graham, whether he liked it or not. It can win for me. I'm not restricted by it. I have the privilege of switching plays when I see a situation I think calls for it. I use about twelve audibles a game. Coach doesn't complain."

Smiling wistfully, Brown, the reformed tyrant, said, "He makes us sort of free-wheeling."

Seemingly, nothing could stifle Cook's brash enthusiasm. It was contagious, spreading to older players who came swiftly to believe in the bold youngster as though he would deliver them to some promised land. Greg would run onto the field, carrying his helmet, his curly locks blowing in the breeze, and call the play in the huddle before he covered his head. After a touchdown he would run off the field, waving a fist triumphantly. From the sidelines, he would dart back on the field briefly to express his pleasure with a veteran's defensive play, frequently whacking the teammate broadly on the backside. In the dressing room, after a triumph over San Diego, he exuded confidence. "We'll beat Kansas City next week, too," he said.

The Kansas City Chiefs were considered the most talented team in the AFL, and indeed they went on to a Super Bowl success. But the Chiefs fell to the Bengals just as Cook had boasted they would. Greg himself threw a 73-yard touchdown pass to Eric Crabtree to ignite a 24-19 upset victory. Later, the Chiefs' big Bobby Bell and Jim Lynch ground him down on a tackle, twisting his throwing arm out of shape. But Cook had set his team on the way to victory before he was sidelined. Pro football is a savage sport, and the quarterbacks are marked men. They are hit as often and as hard as is permissable in order to soften them up and turn the tide. A dozen other passers were also hurt during Cook's rookie year.

"A runner meets a tackle head-on, giving as much punishment as he takes," Cook commented wistfully. "But the passer usually is standing still, perhaps just having released the ball when he is hit. Often, he has been looking elsewhere for his receiver. He doesn't see the blow coming and can't soften it in any way.

"It broke my heart a little when I was hurt because I was going so good, better even than I had expected. But it's part of the game."

Cook fretted through four games before the doctors allowed him to play again. He came back against the awesome Oakland Raiders, who were headed for the Western Division crown. He passed

---

Cook is brought down by Raider Carleton Oats. But the Bengals won 31-17, breaking Oakland's 15-game regular-season winning streak in this 1969 game.

29

his test spectacularly, completing 11 of 19 passes for 189 yards and two touchdowns in a shocking 31-19 upset. The crowd of 27,927 spectators that crammed tiny Nippert Stadium roared its approval. The following week in the Astrodome, Greg was even better, completing 15 of 25 passes for 298 yards and four touchdowns, as the Bengals battled the Oilers to a 31-31 tie.

Cook leveled off somewhat after that. His arm did not seem as strong as it had been before his injury. (Even he admitted it.) But there was no opportunity to rest. He did throw for 291 yards against Denver, but despite this, the Bengals lost the game. During the second half of the season, they lost more games, finishing with a 4-9-1 record. However, the big moments burned bright in Coach Brown's memory and he concluded at season's end that his young team had made promising progress. Having found a quarterback, the coach felt that the future looked good.

The remarkable rookie won the AFL passing championship. With 106 completions in 197 attempts, making a 53.8 percent accuracy average, he gained 1,854 yards, threw 15 touchdown passes and had only 11 passes intercepted. Many purists consider the most valid statistical evidence of a quarterback's ability to be average yards gained per pass attempt. In this category Cook compiled an incredible mark of 9.41 yards a throw, a yard better than his nearest rival.

GREG COOK

A Los Angeles statistical scientist fed the complete statistics on all 1969 quarterbacks (both NFL and AFL) into a computer and announced that the results revealed Cook to be by far the outstanding passer for the year.

Tall enough to see over charging linemen, husky enough to throw hard while being hit, strong enough to bruise a receiver's hands until they swell, and imaginative and confident enough to improvise plays and dissect defenses, Cook looks like the big quarterback of the future.

For some reason, star quarterbacks are frequently strikingly handsome, and Greg Cook is no exception. (Perhaps glamour guys are naturally drawn to the glamour position.) But for all of his brash bounce, Greg is remarkably settled. While a college freshman, he married his high school sweetheart, Deboreh Sholl, and even during his first year as a professional he continued to live in a modest campus apartment with her and a son, Brandon, born in 1967.

Taking advantage of the lucrative opportunities open to him off the field as well as on, Cook started doing public relations work for the Royal Crown Cola soft drink firm and a dry-cleaning company. In addition, he continued his education, working for a degree from the College of Design, Architecture and Art at the University of Cincinnati. He enjoys painting and has considered opening a gallery. "It would be one way of getting my own work on exhibition," he said. Greg works in water colors, mainly.

Clearly an individualist, the massive Greg Cook is a good example for aspiring young athletes.

"Like a lot of fellows, I matured and developed late," he said. "I hate to think of how many potential stars drop out early because they get discouraged along the way or do not fall into the right positions where they get the right opportunities.

"I was pleased by my first year in pro ball, though not entirely satisfied. We won big games early, but not late. Partly, this was due to my injury. The discomfort lingered as long as I had to keep throwing, but I'm sure that with a summer's rest my arm will be as good as ever. My arm is my life right now. I can live with the bad of it as well as the good. They call me 'Confidence Cook.' Well, I expected to do well right away and I did. I expect to do better and I will."

On the basis of what he has done so far, Greg Cook is a man to be believed.

3
Bob
Griese

*Miami Dolphin Bob Griese rests on
the sidelines during a game.*

In a game against the Oakland Raiders during his second pro season, Bob Griese of the Miami Dolphins was able to gain only three first downs on his first three offensive series of plays. The Dolphins were behind, 21-0, on the scoreboard and the crowd in Florida's famous Orange Bowl was booing both the home team and the local hero. Miami, an expansion team in the American Football League, was outclassed by the powerful Oakland club, but this fact did not make its fans less frustrated than those of any other loser.

Weary of battling against long odds and failing week after week, Griese and his teammates returned grimly to what seemed a lost cause. The Raiders had been putting on a furious pass rush. Seeking to take advantage of this, Griese called for a screen-pass on first down. He dropped back and waited calmly for the protection to form in front of the receiver, Larry Csonka, while the burly Raider linemen bore down on him. Then at the last possible moment, just before he was hit and flattened, he unloaded a short toss which Csonka clutched and carried 20 yards to a first down.

Griese got up and called another pass play. With a three-touchdown deficit to make up, the Dolphins could not afford to use up time on a lot of running plays. Griese found a receiver open, but overthrew him. On the next play, he found Csonka open and reached him with a pass, but the receiver dropped it. On third-and-10, Griese called for a pass to Karl Noonan, who was 11 yards away, and succeeded with it for another first down.

The crowd was humming now, its excitement reaching the sweaty athletes in their bulky uniforms on the grassy floor of the great bowl. The Dolphins had reached midfield on two Griese passes. Possibly Oakland was ready for a run now. So Griese called for another pass, a deep one, and flanker Howard Twilly stretched to make a good catch before being downed after a 30-yard gain to the Oakland 20.

Then, Griese called for the run, a draw play to Jim Kiick, who burst through center for 6 yards. Griese went for a touchdown on the next play, but his pass to Noonan was knocked down in the end zone. On third-and-4, the young quarterback tried another pass play, but his receivers were covered so he had to run. Ike Lassiter knocked him out of bounds at the 12, then slammed him with an extra wrench which an official saw. The Raiders were penalized half the distance to the goal line.

38

On first-and-6, the bruised Griese handed off to Csonka for two yards. Then he rolled out to his right, with his pursuers panting after him, and threw back across field to Larry Seiple for a touchdown. The score was now 21-7. The fans stood and cheered, the bands played and the Dolphins' offensive unit trotted off the field happily, feeling they were back in contention.

Oakland then marched 95 yards to make the score 28-7. Griese and his unit had to go back to work to try to make up a 21-point deficit. Gene Milton returned the ensuing kickoff 73 yards, turning the ball over to Griese at the Oakland 27. On first down, Griese was ground into the turf for a 7-yard loss. On second down, he hit Seiple on a pass for 9 yards. On third down, he faked a handoff to Kiick, faded back, then hit Kiick with a pass for a 12-yard gain. But the officials had detected illegal motion and it was nullified. Angrily, Griese used a screen-pass to Kiick, which gained a first down to the Raider 15. Then he pitched to Noonan for 15 yards and a touchdown.

The Raiders came back and scored again. Then they scored again. They overpowered the Dolphin defensive unit to such an extent that Griese and the Dolphin offensive unit could not keep up.

On one play, Griese threw a perfect pass to Kiick. Kiick was late getting his hands up and the ball bounced off his shoulder pads. Oakland's Dave Grayson grabbed it out of the air and returned the "interception" 22 yards before a furious Griese rammed him out of bounds. On another play, Griese hit Noonan with a pass, but the ball bounced off his hands into the air and Oakland's Grayson grabbed it again, returning the ball 23 yards.

As the long afternoon wore on, Griese kept trying. Although he drove the Dolphins to another touchdown, at the final gun they were beaten, 47-21, and their fans booed as the team walked dejectedly off the field.

Griese, boyishly handsome, stripped and sat sadly in the dressing room for a long time before he could rouse his aching body to go to the showers. His skin was damp with sweat, red from exertion and, in many places, black and blue from the punishment he had taken. His shins and hands were scabbed from old sores and skinned by new ones, and a small cut across the bridge of his nose left a trickle of blood running down his face.

"You can't play football when you get so far behind so fast," he told reporters. "In a situation like that, you have to gamble. When a young team gambles, it makes mistakes. I just keep forgetting that we're a young ballclub and don't have the personnel some of the other teams do. I keep thinking we're going to start winning, but we keep right on losing. It's very discouraging and very depressing. We have our pride. All we can do is keep trying and hope for the best."

Eventually, he showered and walked slowly into

the night, where his wife waited to console him. Football may be a game, but it is no fun when you lose, and it was no fun for Bob Griese during his first few years as a professional. His individual performance indicates that had he gone to a top team, he might have become a prominent star by the time the 1960s ran out. On the other hand, had he gone to a top team, he might not have gotten to play so much so soon. As a result, he might well have advanced less, individually.

Football never came easily to Robert Allen Griese, who had a hard road to go on the way to the top. He was born in Evansville, Indiana, on February 3, 1945, one of three children in his family. (The family name is pronounced "Greasy.") There was a brother two years older and a sister two years younger. Their father's death in 1955 was a terrible shock to the children, and Bob seemed especially affected by it. "I've been a quiet person ever since," he has said.

Their mother sold the family plumbing business and went to work as a secretary to support her children. It was a hard struggle for her, but she managed to bring her youngsters up properly. Bob attended Rex Mundi High School. His first year there was also the school's first year, so it did not have strong sports teams. But Bob captained and starred on the football, basketball and baseball teams.

As a senior, he hit .300 and pitched victories in

twelve out of thirteen starts in baseball and was pressured by some scouts to turn pro. But his mother and older brother, who was working hard to help support the family, wanted him to get a college education. Bob agreed. He could afford college on an athletic scholarship.

Although he had gained All-State honors as a football quarterback, Bob threw side-armed and could not get a tight spiral on the ball. Furthermore, he was not very big. He wanted to go to Notre Dame, but school coaches considered him too small. Purdue, however, was interested in him as a possible defensive back. Since he hadn't much choice, Griese agreed to go to the Lafayette, Indiana, school. As a freshman he did play defense, but gradually he fought his way into the offensive quarterback spot.

Griese grew to be only six feet, one inch tall, with a weight of 190 pounds. This is not big as modern quarterback stars go. But he was intelligent and dedicated. He progressed rapidly. One of the reasons he chose Purdue originally was that he was impressed by backfield coach Bob DeMoss, a former quarterback. DeMoss converted Griese to an overhand motion and taught him to spiral the ball. The youngster could soon throw well at most distances, though he lacked long-range power.

Though he was not fast, he was quick with his mind, his feet and his hands. Though he was not strong, he was durable. He did not throw powerfully, but he threw accurately. He also was versatile

—able to run well, punt, kick-off and place-kick. Head coach Jack Mollenkopf dubbed him "The Scholar." He saw in Griese the qualities of inspirational leadership and groomed him for stardom.

Griese started and starred in every game during his three varsity seasons at Purdue. He gained national prominence in three spotlighted contests. He completed 19 passes in 22 attempts—including 13 in a row—for three touchdowns as the Boilermakers upset Notre Dame, 25-21. Bob passed and ran for 169 yards and one touchdown and place-kicked perfectly as Purdue upset otherwise undefeated Michigan, 21-20. And he guided his school to a 14-13 triumph over Southern Cal in the Rose Bowl, Purdue's long-awaited first trip to the Pasadena playground.

During his college career, Griese completed 57 percent of his passes. He completed 348 passes for 4,402 yards and 28 touchdowns. In addition, he scored 249 points running and kicking. He was selected All-America in each of his last two seasons.

In the pro football draft, the new Miami team wanted the University of Florida quarterback Steve Spurrier, who had beaten out Griese for the Heisman Trophy. But San Francisco, drafting ahead of Miami, selected Spurrier so the Dolphins settled for Griese. A confident young man, Griese said, "I've heard about Spurrier, but people in Miami won't be sorry. I've never been with a team I didn't think I could play first-string on. I've heard about the long time it's supposed to take to develop a pro quarter-

Griese carries the ball for Purdue. Michigan State's All-America Bubba Smith (95) comes in for the tackle.

back, but I've got to find out for myself."

Although most new pros were demanding big bonuses, Griese said, "You shouldn't try to bleed anyone. It's silly to ask more than you need to pay your bills. If you get too much, it'll just go in taxes, anyway." Whereupon he held out for six months before signing for a $150,000 bonus. Spurrier got $200,000 from the Forty-Niners. However, as the 1960s ended, Spurrier still was sitting on the San Francisco bench, while Griese was playing regularly in Miami.

In fact, he played regularly right from the beginning of his pro career, though this was highly unexpected. Dolphin coach George Wilson favored another quarterback, John Stofa, who was more experienced. But Stofa suffered a broken ankle in the first five minutes of the first quarter of the Dolphins' first game of the regular 1967 season.

"When they carried him off on a stretcher, I knew he wasn't coming back," Griese recalls. "When Wilson turned to me, I knew I was it. I was scared, but eager. It wasn't a question of if I could do it—I *had* to do it."

Bob went out and completed 12 of 19 passes for two touchdowns. Miami scored a spectacular 32-31 victory. The opening-day crowd gave him a standing ovation as he skipped triumphantly and happily off the field to telephone, as he put it, "all the people who . . . helped me on the way up."

In the next game, Griese was hit so hard on one

46

tackle that he suffered a skull concussion and had to be sidelined. He returned the next week only to be thrown down so hard he smashed his shoulder and was sidelined again. Two weeks later in New York City he came back in the second half of a game and threw 17 completions in 21 attempts for 160 yards and two touchdowns. This was good enough to startle the big-town audience. Although he took a beating during his first three seasons in the majors, he proved himself a true pro.

Miami won four games in 1967, five in 1968 and three in 1969. The 1969 decline can be traced to injuries Griese suffered. First he had a bruised knee, then bruised ribs, then a twisted elbow. Finally torn cartilage in his knee sidelined him for the last five games. Owner Joe Robbie said, "We just are not the same team without his magic." Coach Wilson commented, "He's our number one strong point. I wouldn't trade him for any quarterback in the AFL, and that includes Joe Namath." Wilson added, ". . . considering Namath's two bad knees, of course."

Griese now has one bad knee and Wilson has been replaced as coach by Don Shula. But Shula's great quarterback at Baltimore, John Unitas, gave Griese a tip as to how the new coach regards him when he said, "Griese is the best young quarterback in pro football."

The team doctor recommended an operation to repair his knee, but Griese sought the advice of other physicians. He accepted that of Dr. Frank Reynolds of St. Louis, who prescribed exercises used by Len Dawson. The treatment enabled Dawson to come back in 1969 and lead Kansas City to a Super Bowl success. "I kept seeing doctors until I found one who told me what I wanted to hear." Griese smiled.

Bob is confident and articulate, as well as calculating and quiet. "Nothing ever seems to excite me much," he admits. "I just never have been the rah-rah type." While in Honolulu for the Hula Bowl game after his final college game, he and a teammate went swimming and were sucked out to sea by an undertow. Bob tried to help his floundering friend and soon both were in trouble. Natives had to pull them out. On his return, Griese announced his engagement to Judi Ann Lassus of Fort Wayne.

"I had a close call. I'm not going to take any more chances of missing anything in life," he said, smiling calmly.

He gave up ocean swimming and was married to Judi in June of 1967. They now have a son, Robert, Jr., and a home in Coral Gables.

In three seasons he completed more than half of his passes—473, to be exact, for 6,173 yards and 40 touchdowns despite poor support. Demonstrating their faith in Griese, the Dolphins obtained Paul Warfield, the great Cleveland flanker, by giving up their first draft choice in 1969. This enabled the

Browns to pick Griese's All-American quarterback successor at Purdue, Mike Phipps, but it also bolstered Bob's support.

Griese's accuracy is attested by two league records he has set. He established a one-game record by completing 82 percent of his passes, 17 of 21, in a game against the Jets in New York in 1967. That same season he set an all-time mark by throwing 122 consecutive passes without an interception. He also threw touchdown passes in nine straight games.

His biggest asset appears to be his coolness and his quick release. Although his mates have not provided him with the protection of stronger teams, he is able to wait until the last possible moment to throw because he throws so swiftly. He does not have the arm of a Roman Gabriel or a Greg Cook, but he insists, "The most important thing in a quarterback is intelligent leadership, not a great arm. I am not a great advocate of the long pass, anyway. I wasn't brought up to be a hit-or-miss player. I don't want to build my team up to a big letdown. I prefer to move a team systematically down the field, controlling the ball."

He admits he is striving to overcome the temptation to force passes through tight defenses, though rival safetyman Ken Houston of the Houston Oilers praises him for this, saying, "He's confident and bold and never afraid to throw. Even more than Namath, he'll stick the ball in there."

Despite his youth, Griese is a firm leader who per-

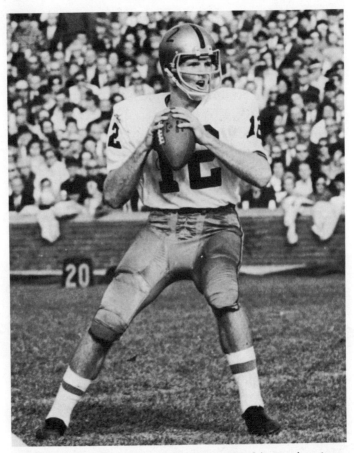

Bob, in a Purdue uniform, demonstrates his passing form.

mits no one else to talk in the huddle and has told veterans who tried to do so to "shut up." A student of strategy, he says, "Football is like playing chess; you're only as good as your next move." He says, "It's simple really. Pro football players are the best.

You look for the worst of the best and try to beat
them. If you find a defensive back who is not quite
as good as the others, you work on him, for
example." Once when he was accused of throwing to
one end, Jack Clancy, too much, Griese said, "When

you find a good tree, you keep going back for the fruit."

He is considered a scrambler, although he says he runs only when he does not have a good alternative. Still, he has averaged five yards a run and Baltimore's Bubba Smith, who has been chasing him since Big Ten days, groans, "I haven't tackled him yet." Because of lack of support, Griese has had to scramble a lot and has been exposed to injuries which threaten his future. However, he says, "I don't worry about injuries because I don't let myself think about them. The most important thing for me is landing on a team that could let me play right away."

He points out, "There are two ways to learn my position. You can watch movies and sit on the bench and study a Starr, a Unitas or a Dawson, or you can play and learn by doing, making your own mistakes and profiting by them, finding your own way. The second way is the best way and I have been fortunate it could be my way."

Smiling wistfully, he comments, "Since the death of my father, it has been a struggle for me. I do not have the size or arm of some who play my position, but I've worked hard to make the most of myself. I've always had the desire to be the best, but when I look at what I've accomplished so far, I'm surprised. Still, I feel I have a long way to go and I long for the day I can lead a contender. You can't live in the past. You always have to look to the future."

4
Sonny Jurgensen

Sonny Jurgensen has long been considered the finest pure passer in football. Through the end of the 1960s, he twice led the NFL in touchdown passes, four times in total completion and five times in yards gained by passing. In 1967, he set new single-season statistical records in most major departments of passing. In 1969, at the advanced age of 35, he led the league in passing for the second time in his career.

Yet Jurgensen has slipped through the shadows almost unnoticed. The fans, the writers, the other players and the coaches all know about his talents. But they don't seem to spend much time thinking about him. He is accepted as though he was some monument. This is probably because he seldom has played on a winning team and never has led a championship team. He has the statistics of an all-time immortal, but he never has been selected All-Pro.

After thirteen frustrating years in the pro leagues, he may find his situation changing in the 1970s, providing he holds up physically. A playboy in his youth, he has become a solid citizen in his maturity and has come under the guidance of Vince Lombardi. The former Green Bay coach raised the standing of the Washington Redskins enormously during his first season as coach of the club. He promised to put together the first winning team ever to surround Jurgensen.

"I've waited a long time to play on a winner," Sonny says. "I was just a fun-loving boy who went my own way for a while, but I don't think it ever hurt my performances on the football field. We all need help and there were times I didn't have much. Now I feel I'll get help and it's up to me to prove myself. My chance is coming late, but not too late, I hope.

"I still feel good and strong and coach Lombardi seems to have confidence in me. I'd like to repay that confidence. He's a very inspiring man. I've had my share of disappointments in my career. Not individually. I don't worry about awards. Team-wise, though, I'd like to have won more. It's been a long, hard way I've gone."

Christian Adolph Jurgensen was born August 23, 1934, in Wilmington, North Carolina. A natural, all-around athlete, he won a tennis tournament a month after he took up the sport. At New Hanover High School, he starred in football, basketball and baseball (preceding Roman Gabriel as the school's gridiron star). He was good enough in baseball to be offered a pro contract by the Athletics, but he preferred football.

During his junior year, he was a middle linebacker on defense and a running halfback on offense, but in his senior year he switched to quarterback and swiftly accelerated as a passer. "Our coach, Leon Brogden, had a drill in which I had to get on one knee and throw the ball," Sonny recalled. "It may not seem like much, but I think it developed the strength in my arm and taught me how to really snap the ball the way I do."

He was offered a number of college scholarships and accepted one from Duke University in his home state of North Carolina. Coach Bill Murray's Blue Devils were oriented toward a running game, however. Although Jurgensen helped them to twenty victories, three ties and only eight defeats—plus a 34-7 conquest of Nebraska in an Orange Bowl appearance—he was not permitted to pass frequently enough to demonstrate much potential in this area.

During his sophomore season, Jurgensen completed 12 of 28 passes for 212 yards. As a junior he completed 37 of 39 passes for 536 yards, and as a senior, 29 of 59 passes for 371 yards. He had just six touchdown passes during his college career. While he was not named to any All-America teams, Sonny was somehow spotted by Philadelphia Eagle scouts. The Eagles selected him on the fourth round of the pro draft prior to the 1957 season.

Jurgensen is another example of an outstanding player who developed late. It is unusual for an athlete who has not been a college star to become an exceptional pro star, but Jurgensen is an exception to the rule. For four seasons in Philadelphia—under Hugh Devore for one year, then Buck Shaw for three years—he sat on the bench or stood at the sidelines with earphones connected to the "spotters" on the roof.

He threw as few as five passes during one full season and as many as 70 during another season. He went into games that were already won or lost by wide margins. In his first two seasons, these games were usually lost since Philadelphia had a mediocre team. But after Norm Van Brocklin arrived, through trades with the Rams, the Eagles improved and began to win. They tied for second place in the Eastern Division in 1959 and won the division and the title play-off against Green Bay in 1960.

Jurgensen played little part in these triumphs, however, and it depressed him deeply. He made up for his disappointment by seeking fun on the outside. A naturally carefree soul with a mop of reddish hair and a ready grin, Sonny is a friendly fellow who likes to laugh.

During his period of relative inactivity on the playing field, Jurgensen found it hard to be serious about his sport, in which he seldom saw action. Although he partied a good deal, in a more serious moment he said he especially wanted to make good for the sake of his parents. "My father worked hard to give me an opportunity," he said. "My mother has always been encouraging." In college, his mother used to write him letters of tactical advice. "When they bunch up in the middle, run around the ends," she wrote him once. With such suggestions, he was bound to succeed eventually.

The cocky, calloused Van Brocklin may unwittingly have spurred Sonny to fame when he publicly proclaimed him "a clown." Pete Retzlaff, then an Eagle teammate, now an Eagle executive, said that few ever realized how much that description hurt the happy-go-lucky youngster. "It almost turned him into a recluse, but filled him with burning desire," Retzlaff recalls.

Then Van Brocklin retired as an Eagle player to become coach of the new Minnesota team, and Nick Skorich took over from Buck Shaw as head coach in 1961. The years of waiting were finally over and Jurgensen got his chance to establish himself. Eventually he would surpass many of Van Brocklin's best records.

In his first full season, Jurgensen was spectacular. He completed more than 56 percent of his passes for an average of nearly nine yards an attempt. He led the league in completions (235), yards gained (3,723), and touchdown passes (32). But he also led in passes intercepted with 24. The free-throwing lad also almost led the Eagles to another title. Their

10-4-0 record fell just a half-game short of New York's 10-3-1, in the NFL's Eastern Division.

At the time Jurgensen didn't know that that was the closest he would come to a crown for the rest of the decade. He was a young man playing with an old team that was on the decline. The following season he slipped only slightly to 196 completions for 3,261 yards and 22 touchdowns, again leading the league in passes intercepted with 26. The Eagles skidded into the cellar at 3-10-1. They remained in the cellar the next season at 2-10-2 for Jurgensen missed a good deal of playing time because of an injury.

During this low period, Jurgensen was blamed for many of the Eagles' problems. The "experts" said he was a flashy performer who passed behind his back one time and left-handed under pressure several times. They also claimed he passed too much, often forcing passes through tight defenses. Plagued with weak ankles, Jurgensen was not a good runner or an agile workman. Because he had the reputation of partying too much, and because he was overweight, the fans thought he was out of shape. When the Eagles lost, they blamed him. Often he was booed.

"Well, here it is again, fellows," he once said as the fans yelled at him. "You've got 60,000 critics and no private life in this game. I don't let it eat my in-

---

Jurgensen shows his ability to get off a pass when under pressure and off-balance.

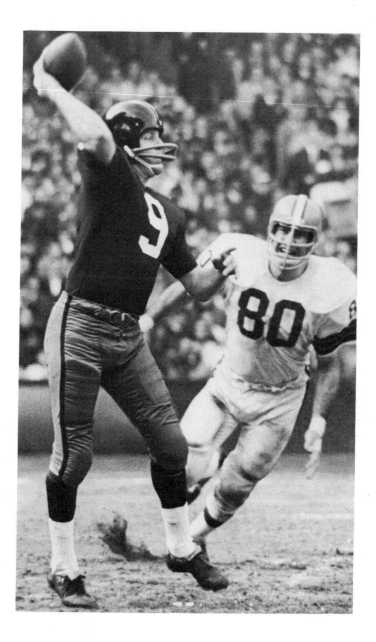

sides out." However, teammate Tim Brown said, "He never let on, but it hurt."

Some of Sonny's own teammates were unsure of him. After all, they were losing with him. Jurgensen recalls, "I remember when I broke in and called a play. A veteran asked me, 'Hey, rookie, do you think this is going to work?' I said, 'Yes, or I wouldn't have called it. It better work.' After a while I found out I had to say, 'You're darned right it will work.' If you don't have confidence in a play, the others won't, and they won't go at it so it'll work. If they don't do their jobs, you can't do yours. They have to believe in you. But your teammates have to respect you as a person as well as a player if you're going to be a leader."

Respect did not come to Jurgensen in Philadelphia, but it did later in Washington as he matured. Joe Kuharich became the new coach of the Eagles and cleaned house, sweeping out Sonny in a trade to the Redskins for Norm Snead. Kuharich was to last five years before being fired because the Eagles were back in the basement at 2-12. Meanwhile the Redskins struggled with Jurgensen—6-8 two years in a row, then 7-7, 5-6-3 and 5-9. Although the win-loss records were mediocre, Jurgy compiled some of the most astonishing passing records in history.

The 6-foot, 205-pounder was a quarterback in the old mold, chunky rather than rangy. But he was tough and he could throw a perfect spiral—soft or hard, short or long—with uncanny accuracy. Although he sometimes suffered from sore elbows, he shook off punishment and pain to do a job against opposition that outclassed his support.

He completed 207 passes for 2,934 yards and 24 scores in 1964 and 190 passes for 2,367 yards and 15 scores in 1965. (Part of the time he was sidelined by injuries.) In 1966, he came into his own. That year he set league records by completing 254 of 436 passes (more than 58 percent) for 3,209 yards, at the same time throwing 28 touchdown passes.

In 1967, he surpassed these new standards with 288 completions in 508 attempts (more than 56 percent) for 3,747 yards, and set a fourth mark with 31 touchdown passes. His interceptions, which had been dropping to half his early number, were only 16.

During the summer of 1968, he had an elbow operation for removal of calcium deposits in the joint, so he did not play until the final preseason game. Then, after the fifth game of the regular season, it was discovered he had fractured ribs. A special protective case was made for him, which he had to wear, uncomfortably, for the rest of the season. Finally, he was felled by the flu. In all, he missed three full games and parts of others, but he finished with 167 completions out of 292 tries for 1,980 yards, 17 touchdown passes and only 11 interceptions.

By the time Lombardi came on the scene in 1969,

With Bear defenders rushing from all sides, Sonny throws.

Jurgensen was aging, but healthy again. There were those who felt the dedicated, stern Lombardi would not be able to tolerate the carefree Jurgensen. Furthermore, almost everyone expected Lombardi to shift the emphasis to running. But Lombardi found Jurgensen a changed man and, recognizing real talent when he saw it, stuck to a passing attack as his best weapon in rebuilding the Redskins.

In 1969, Jurgensen completed more than 62 percent of his passes, 274 of 442 for 3,102 yards—all league highs. He threw 22 touchdown passes and had only 15 intercepted as he secured his second passing crown. "He seems as good as ever, which is about as good as they come," commented Lombardi.

At his best, Jurgensen always has been someone to reckon with. His longest completions each season have included passes of 61, 61, 71, 75, 80, 84, 86, 86, 88 and a league record of 99 yards. He threw touchdown passes in 23 straight games. In a game against Washington in 1961, he completed 27 of 41 passes for 436 yards and two touchdowns. In one against Dallas in 1965, he completed 26 of 42 for 411 yards and three touchdowns. In back-to-back games in 1967, he completed 32 passes for 418 yards and three touchdowns against Cleveland one week; then the next week he completed 30 for 366 yards and four touchdowns against Philadelphia. But despite his playing, the Redskins lost, 42-37, to Cleveland and settled for a tie, 35-35, with Philadelphia.

"It's great when you win, but it eats you up inside

when you lose," Jurgensen said. "Winning is the thing that counts. It is the only goal worth reaching for. All other things have to be secondary. Whatever I've done has not been enough so far."

What Jurgensen has done, however, is exceptional in football history. Through the end of the 1960s, he

---

Sonny talks with Redskin spotters who watch the game from high in the stands.

had five times completed more than 200 passes and gained more than 3,000 yards in single seasons; and in thirteen seasons he had completed nearly 2,000 of approximately 3,500 passes for nearly 27,000 yards and 213 touchdowns. This placed him among the top two or three all-time leaders in most respects. He had completed more than 55 percent of his passes.

Fame, fortune and titles may come fast for a Joe Namath, but for a Sonny Jurgensen—despite his colorful personality and proven ability—these can remain elusive for a long time, if not forever. "If I had known how frustrating it would be," he said, "I might have gone another way. But football can be fun and it's the thing I do best, so I have few regrets."

Considered "old" by present-day standards, and a bit paunchy now, he remains colorful and brilliant, a key figure on Vince Lombardi's new crusade for victory in our nation's capital. Jurgensen is not booed in D.C. Stadium. Instead, he is revered as the leader of a renaissance.

"When Van Brocklin called me a clown, it hurt me," the new leader says. "When I waited long years for my chance, then was pressured by the public, it depressed me. Over the years, defeats have embittered me. But you can't be a coward and quit.

"Lombardi has given me a new lease on life. I'm no kid, but I'm trying like one."

5
Joe Namath

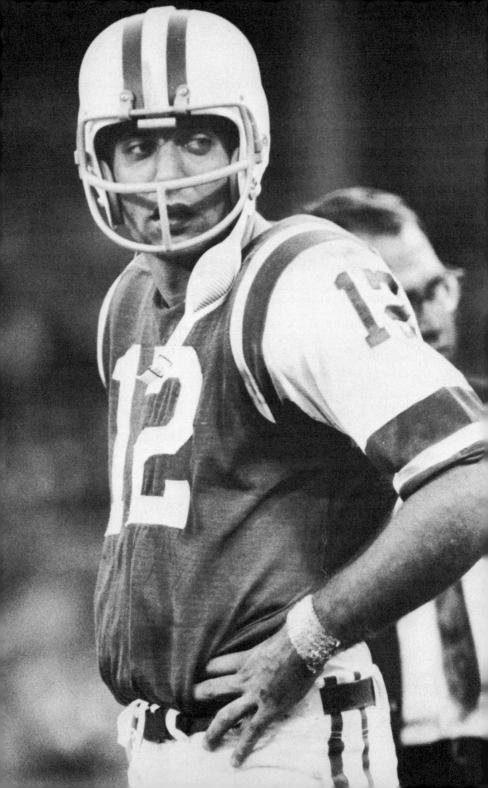

Joe Willie Namath said that he and his New York Jets would win the 1969 Super Bowl and they did. He also said there were five or six AFL quarterbacks, including himself, who were superior to the Baltimore Colts' surprise star, Earl Morall; and by the time the Super Bowl game was over the fans believed him.

The Colts had won thirteen of fourteen games during the regular season, then mauled the Minnesota Vikings and clobbered the Cleveland Browns in the NFL play-offs. The Baltimore team had the toughest defense in pro football, and the previously undistinguished Morrall had replaced the sore-armed Johnny Unitas to give them a spectacular offense.

In the first two Super Bowl contests, the NFL champion Green Bay Packers had badly beaten the AFL champions. Thus the new NFL kings, the Colts, were 18-point favorites to whip the AFL Jets in the third confrontation between the two rival leagues.

71

But the cocky and controversial playboy, Joe Willie Namath, operating on two bad legs, made the best of his good arm. And in perhaps the most dramatic upset in pro football history, he overcame the odds to place his upstart league on a level with the old league, thereby establishing himself as something of an immortal.

The facts are that until that sunny afternoon in Florida in January of 1969, the "$400,000 quarterback" had been something of a flop. He was intercepted frequently, even by weak opponents, and his team had folded in the stretch several seasons in succession. He was considered a clown and his team was thought to be one which "choked" in the clutch.

However, by staggering to the divisional pennant and then upsetting Oakland in the play-off, Joe and the Jets had their chance at glory and $25,000 in individual bonuses in Miami's Orange Bowl. A crowd of 75,000 fans convened to see the slaughter, while millions of television viewers across the country tuned in. The stage was set, and Broadway Joe performed to perfection.

The Colts seemed on the verge of knocking out the Jets early in the game but they were unable to connect with a good punch. On a typical play, Morrall hit end Tom Mitchell with a perfect pass in the end zone, but the ball bounced off Mitchell's shoulder and the Jets took over. Namath ran fullback Matt Snell several times, and then began to throw. Varying both his length of passes and his patterns, Joe connected to Bill Mathis, George Sauer and Snell to put the ball inside the Baltimore 10. From there Snell bulled over to score. The crowd stood and cheered in surprise, but few believed that the lead would last.

It did. Namath was unable to score again for a while, but he avoided the rush of the Colts' powerful defensive linemen, picked apart the Colts' defensive backfield and maintained constant control of the ball. When the Colts got the pigskin, they were helpless. Late in the half, Baltimore's Tom Matte broke loose and burst 58 yards to New York's 16-yard line, but then John Sample of the Jets intercepted a pass by Morrall in the end zone. The Jets were still ahead, 7-0, at the half.

The bands played and the fans waited for the bubble to burst. But the bubble which burst was Baltimore's, punctured by the sharp jabs of Joe Namath. After the teams resumed play, Matte fumbled, the Jets recovered and Namath moved them to a field goal by Jim Turner to make the score 10-0. A little later, the Jets got the ball back, and Namath marched them to another field goal and a 13-0 lead.

When the Colts thought Namath would call a pass, he handed off on a run. When they expected a run, he passed. He passed short and long. He passed to the left and to the right. While he was not spectacular, he gave a textbook demonstration on the art of quarterbacking that thrilled the purists. He guided the Jets on another drive, which included a perfect pass for 39 yards to flanker George Sauer. Soon the Jets had another field goal and an insurmountable 16-0 lead.

By then, Unitas had replaced Morrall and the veteran took Baltimore 80 yards to a touchdown, cutting the Colt deficit to 16-7. But less than four minutes remained, and at the end, after another Colt drive had stalled, Namath ran out the clock.

Broadway Joe and his Jets whooped and hollered. They danced into the dressing room. In the winners' quarters, the happy sounds were not just those of another team title. They represented the sudden discovery of a league's equality. "I guess we lived up to my boasts," Joe said, laughing.

As Joe Namath's father hugged him in tearful triumph, Jet coach Weeb Ewbank said, "Mr. Namath, you have a remarkable son."

Joseph William Namath was born May 31, 1943, in Beaver Falls, Pennsylvania, in the heart of one of America's best prep football breeding grounds. Joe's father worked in a steel mill. Once, when his son was 12, the father took him to the mill to see it. "It was hot and dirty and all that noise. It scared me half to death," Joe recalls. "I never went back there after that one time—never."

Joe throws to his Jet receiver in the 1969 Super Bowl. Baltimore's Mike Curtis (32) is too late for the tackle.

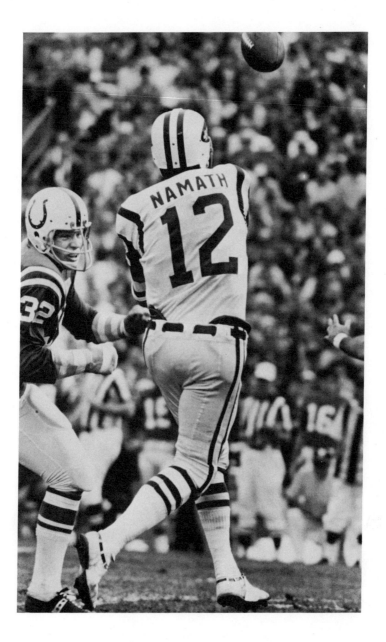

Joe's parents were divorced when he was young, and he and two older brothers were raised by their mother. They were a poor family in a struggling town. When he was young, Joe shined shoes for fifty cents a week and tips. He was a wild, tough kid, but he was never in major trouble. Mrs. Namath says, "As a mother, I can see he did a lot of mischievous things growing up. He did 'boy things.' But Joey always has been a good boy."

He was a very thin boy, who liked to play football with his older brothers. But he was cut from his junior high school team and high school varsity. After he was not chosen while a sophomore, as one of his school's 50 best players for a special summer camp session, he went to coach Bill Ross and said, "I think I should quit! I'm too small. I'm not getting any place."

But Ross said, "You'll grow. Think it over before giving up."

Joe didn't give up. And throughout the stories of many athletes who became stars there runs this thread of early failure. Many require additional growth and maturity before they reach their potential.

In Namath's case he grew three inches taller and added 25 pounds between his sophomore and junior years in high school. He added three more inches and 25 more pounds between his junior and senior years. By the time he graduated, he was a 6-foot, 185-pounder. He progressed from an alternate varsity quarterback to an All-State selection.

Joe has big hands, a strong arm and quick reflexes. Despite a shoulder separation suffered during his last year in high school, he became one of the most sought-after college prospects in the country.

He had a problem, though, because his marks were not outstanding. After visiting several campuses, he chose to attend the University of Maryland. But twice he failed the entrance examination. Recommended to coach Paul "Baer" Bryant at the University of Alabama, Joe agreed to go south. There he joined a "football factory" with a long record of gridiron success.

As a Northerner off the streets of a small, hard Pennsylvania town, he at first seemed out of place in the genteel South. He was something of a loner until he gradually won acceptance for his football ability. Within the fraternity of athletes, he felt more comfortable.

As a sophomore at Alabama, Namath played a great deal and the team lost only one game. The lone defeat, to Georgia Tech by just one point, was a distressing setback for it ended a 27-game undefeated streak. By the season's end, however, Joe was a star in a 17-0 triumph over Oklahoma in the Orange Bowl.

But he had problems at the Tuscaloosa school. After hours one night he crashed a car into a tree on a rain-slick highway. Then late in his junior season, during which Alabama lost to Auburn and Florida, he was seen drinking in town. Coach Bryant suspended him from the team. That meant Joe would miss another bowl appearance. Other players were involved in the drinking episode, but they had not been identified by the informant, nor would Joe name them. Thus they escaped punishment. When coach Bryant told Joe's mother about the episode, she wept and pleaded for mercy for him. Other friends rallied to his support. At first, Namath was angry and prepared to quit school, but friends calmed him down. Joe apologized to Bryant and was welcomed back for his senior season.

In 1964, Joe and Steve Sloan alternated at quarterback. They led Alabama to an undefeated campaign. However, during an October game against North Carolina State, Joe rolled out on a pass play, twisted his right knee and collapsed in pain. He did not return to the lineup that day, though he played in later games.

Sloan started the Orange Bowl against Texas, but Namath took over after Texas had gotten a 14-0 lead. Although his injured knee was encased in a brace, Joe fought hard, and his passing brought the Crimson Tide back into the game. With seven seconds to play, Texas led, 21-17, but Namath had Alabama on the Texas 1-yard line. On the last play of the game, Namath tried to sneak over, but was stopped short by Tommy Nobis.

Despite this disappointing conclusion to his college career, Namath had gained 255 yards passing on one good leg that night and was hailed as the most outstanding pro prospect to come along in many years. The St. Louis Cardinals of the NFL and the Jets of the AFL entered into a bidding war for him.

Sonny Werblin, a co-owner of the Jets and a veteran of the entertainment world, believed in "the star system" as the best way to popularize the team and the young league. He was willing to pay a great deal for the glamorous college star. Finally, he offered Joe a complicated contract calling for $400,000 for four seasons. Joe accepted and swept into the big town on a wave of publicity. His contract set a precedent which swelled the bonus demands of the many top collegians and hastened the merger of the rival leagues.

But the large salary created a problem for Joe in training camp. Some veteran players on the Jets resented the fact that this untried youngster was making so much more money than they were. It did not help his standing with them when he turned out to be a cocky character who spoke arrogantly to the press and led a carefree bachelor's life, escorting pretty girls through the famous night clubs of the big city. "I just do what I want to do," he said with a shrug.

Namath treated his teammates well, however, and

Joe finds it difficult to avoid injury when defenders head for him on every play. Here Detroit Lions Alex Karras (71) and Joe Robb (84) charge him in an exhibition game.

gradually won them over. His colorful life style became less important to them than his exceptional ability. He and coach Ewbank clashed frequently because of Joe's eccentric training habits and his disinterest in dull training routines, but Namath eventually won Ewbank over, too.

Namath had had an operation on his leg prior to his rookie season. Other operations would follow, for both knees were injured and reinjured as he continued to play. But he performed with courage and did not miss a game in his first five pro seasons. He resented writers' questions about his knees and he never asked for sympathy.

With Namath at the helm, the Jets gradually improved from 5-8-1 in 1965, to 6-6-2 in 1966, and 8-5-1 in 1967. During 1967 Namath's stature grew. He set league records by completing 258 of 491 passes for 4,007 yards and 26 touchdowns.

Off the field, Namath's popularity grew, too. He cultivated a drooping Fu Manchu mustache, then a beard which he shaved off for a television commercial (and a $10,000 fee). He wore white shoes on the field and a $5,000 mink coat off it. He opened an East Side bar in Manhattan and generally lived the high life. Meanwhile, his critics said that Joe's antics were hurting his football game.

In the early part of the 1968 season, the critics had further reason to complain. In one game, Buffalo players intercepted five of Joe's passes and returned three of them for touchdowns. The fact that Joe threw four TD passes of his own did not offset the errors, and the Buffalo Bills recorded a 37-35 upset. (They never won another game all year long.) Two weeks later Denver—never a threat—intercepted Joe five times and defeated the Jets, 21-13.

In twelve other games, however, Namath was intercepted only seven times and his team lost only once. The Jets captured their first Eastern Division crown.

Because his bad legs kept him from running, Joe was forever subjected to severe pounding by the opposition. But he persevered. He got back quicker and set up farther back than most quarterbacks and revealed a faster and stronger arm than most. He was getting quite a reputation among the experts as a "pure" passer.

In the AFL play-off, he demonstrated his other unique qualities—tactical judgment and leadership. Before 62,627 spectators in New York's Shea Stadium, he was magnificent against heavily favored Oakland. He threw three times to flanker Don Maynard, the last time for a touchdown and an early 7-0 lead. Then Joe directed a drive to a field goal that boosted the score to 10-0 by the end of the quarter. Quarterback Daryle Lamonica led Oakland to a touchdown that made it 10-7, but Namath matched him with drives to field goals that left the lead at 13-10, at intermission.

In the second half, Namath and Lamonica matched wits until the Raiders had a 23-20 edge

with time running out. Namath rose to the occasion, however, with a 52-yard pass play to Maynard that carried the ball to the Oakland 6-yard line and a short pass to Maynard that won the game, 27-23.

The crowd, the largest ever to see an AFL title game, cheered Joe and the Jets off the field and into the Super Bowl, where they scored their momentous upset. For the 1969 season, Namath was acclaimed as the MVP in the American Football League and the outstanding performer in all of football.

Quick to capitalize on his success, Joe opened a chain of restaurants, got his own television show, wrote his autobiography and became perhaps the most controversial celebrity in sports. With his longish hair and mod clothes, he was considered a superswinger.

Prior to the 1969 season, however, Namath was censured by pro football commissioner Pete Rozelle for associating with gamblers in his club. While Joe was not charged with any wrong himself, such associations cast suspicion on him. Joe retired from the game in a tearful press conference that followed an ultimatum from Rozelle to sell his interest in his club or be suspended.

Soon afterward, Namath renounced his retirement and agreed to sell his restaurant. Then he set

---

One of Namath's great strengths is his ability to call the right play.

out to prove that football came first with him. During the 1969 season the Jets were once more the Eastern Division champions of the AFL, but they were beaten by Kansas City, 13-6, in the league play-offs. Namath failed on 26 of 40 passes.

Individually, Namath had had a respectable season. He completed more than half his passes, 185, for 2,734 yards and 19 touchdowns.

The statistics for Namath's first five years as a pro show that he has completed more than 1,000 passes for more than 15,000 yards and 97 touchdowns. He twice led the league in attempts, completions and yardage and twice averaged more than eight yards per pass. However, he also completed less than half his attempts in three different seasons and twice led the league in interceptions. Still, Vince Lombardi has said, "He is the best." And Al Davis has said, "He tilts the field."

The outstanding player in the league all-star games of 1965 and 1967 and the main star of the league's most dramatic triumph, Namath remained a most controversial character as pro football entered a new era in the 1970s. His knees were so bad that he had trouble walking off the field, though he often played to perfection on it.

Joe Namath's future in football was clearly in doubt—more so than in the past. But he did not look forward to retirement. "When I leave the game," he says, "it may hurt me more than my knees do."

6
Craig Morton

Morton winces with pain as he takes a jarring tackle from Cleveland's Jack Gregory.

In an exhibition game prior to the 1969 season, quarterback Craig Morton of the Dallas Cowboys slammed his throwing hand against an opponent's helmet on the follow-through of a pass. The impact dislocated his right index finger. Doctors said they could not straighten it out without resorting to surgery, which Morton did not want. The finger was swollen and bent in the shape of a hook. "It's curved just right," said Craig, with a grin. "It fits right around the football." On the third Sunday of the regular season, Morton completed 14 of 18 passes for 261 yards and three touchdowns against Philadelphia, bad finger and all.

The following Sunday against Atlanta, after Morton rolled out to throw a pass to the opposite side of the field, he was hit from his blind side by a crushing tackle. He came down on his right (throwing) shoulder, wrenching it apart. The shoulder separation was strapped up and the next week against Philadelphia, Morton connected on 13 of 19 passes for 247 yards and five touchdowns.

89

Following the game, Ray Berry, an assistant coach for Dallas, said to the other players, "Hey, guys, let's all jump on Morton and beat him up so he'll be ready for next week."

Like so many others, Craig Morton had waited a long time to become a regular quarterback in pro football. He sat on the bench for four years. Then when he did begin to play regularly, in his fifth season, he was virtually torn apart by his opponents. However, he was not inclined to surrender his opportunity. By midseason, he was leading the league in passing with an incredible completion percentage of more than 71 percent. In addition, he had thrown no interceptions, and his yardage totals were impressive.

As the season wore on, the shoulder worsened. "I couldn't practice and I played in pain," he said. "Every quarterback has bread-and-butter plays, which he knows he can complete most of the time —not touchdown plays, but first-down plays. I couldn't practice enough with my receivers to get my timing down and I lost these." Still, Morton wound up with a 53 percent completion figure for 302 attempts. He gained 2,619 yards and threw 21 touchdown passes. Dallas wound up with an imposing 11-2-1 record and the Capitol Division championship.

Morton was ineffective, however, in the NFL play-offs against the Cleveland Browns. He could no longer throw a strong spiral and he was intercepted twice (one of the interceptions was returned 88 yards for a touchdown). The Cowboys were stampeded, 38-14.

For the fourth straight season, the Dallas team seemed headed for a championship, only to fail when the play-offs began. Morton, as the quarterback, was in the hot seat, even though he was in his first season as a starter. But he wasn't about to become a lonesome cowboy. "I can stand the heat," he told reporters, who would relay the word to his critics. "I've worked too hard and too long to let success get away from me now."

For Craig Morton the past began in Flint, Michigan, where he was born February 5, 1943. When he was four, his family moved to Campbell, California, not too far from San Francisco. Craig was reared there. His father, Kenneth, is a glass blower who produces and repairs neon signs among other things. He now has his own shop in San Jose. Craig was the first child, followed by two sisters. His father encouraged him in sports. The older Morton had been a good enough catcher in his own youth to have had a pro baseball tryout.

Morton grew early and matured rapidly. He won All-State honors in baseball and basketball as well as football. He was tempted by baseball bonus bids right up to the time he signed a pro football contract, but he had suffered knee injuries which affected his form at the plate.

As a junior at Campbell High, Craig was 6 feet 2 inches tall but he weighed only 170 pounds. He was an impressive athlete, but not consistent. By the time his senior year arrived, he had added an inch and 15 pounds. He became an awesome runner as well as a fine passer. His team went undefeated, and in the annual Shrine All-Star Game in the Coliseum in Los Angeles, he connected on an 88-yard scoring pass to bring the North a rare victory in its series with the South.

Many colleges sought him, but he chose the University of California at Berkeley. As a freshman, he led the Pacific Eight yearlings in running as well as passing, but the following fall he injured his right knee on the first day of varsity practice so he was able to play only occasionally that year. In his first start, he set a single-game school record by passing for 276 yards in a 23-21 upset of a fine Penn State team.

Cal did not have much other talent while Morton was there; her teams took a back seat to USC and UCLA. The Golden Bears had two 3-7 seasons, a 5-5 year despite their fine quarterbacking. Craig was uncommonly advanced for a collegian, able to throw all kinds of passes with accuracy. Most passers take a long time to develop versatility, but early in his career Morton could throw any pass dictated by a given situation.

Coach Ray Willsey installed a pro-type offense to take advantage of Morton's pro-type talents. As a senior, Craig completed 60 percent of his passes for 2,121 yards and 13 touchdowns. He concluded his college career with 4,501 yards passing and 36 touchdowns, one of the top performances in NCAA history. He was named to the All-American team.

Confident, athletic and handsome, he was a "Big Man on Campus" in the truest sense. The first youngster to write him for his autograph received a reply of such graciousness, inviting him to be Craig's guest at a game, that the lad's mother submitted it to a newspaper. The paper printed it, publicly acclaiming Morton's gentlemanly manner.

On the field, he demonstrated similar poise despite defeats. After Utah defeated California, Coach Ray Nagel called Morton, "The best college quarterback I've ever seen." After Illinois beat the Golden Bears, Illini coach Pete Elliott called him, "The biggest throwing threat in years."

After the latter game, Illini linebacker star Dick Butkus said, "Morton always looked at the guy he was going to throw to and I knew every time where the ball was going." Apparently it didn't do him much good, for Craig completed 24 of 34 passes for 251 yards, narrowly missing a last-second touchdown that would have averted a 20-14 loss.

Morton was drafted off the top of the college ranks by both Dallas of the NFL and Oakland of the AFL. He chose to go to Dallas for a bonus estimated to be in excess of $100,000. Here, he and fellow rookie Jerry Rhome, an All-America from SMU, found themselves trapped behind veteran regular Don Meredith.

Pro coaches like to have quality prospects waiting in the wings to relieve the stars in case of injury and to replace them in case of retirement. But for consistency's sake, coaches prefer to go with one regular in order to develop a consistent pattern of play. The reserves don't like it, but there is not much they can do.

Morton's early problems at Dallas were multiplied by injuries. He hurt a knee in practice before his first season of pro ball—his left knee this time. A third operation left him with only one of two cartilages in each joint. The operations nullified his reputation as a lethal runner, but he still remained a prime passing prospect. He studied movies, manned the telephones on the bench, and was tutored by Meredith and Dallas coach Tom Landry. He even became friendly with Meredith. In time Morton beat out Rhome as the number two man and in the infrequent opportunities offered him, he tried hard to impress his superiors.

He played briefly in four games during his first year, six his second, ten his third and thirteen his fourth. Although he completed half his passes, he had only 143 completions for 2,128 yards after four seasons. Every year he went to camp determined to beat out Meredith, and coach Landry promised he

---

Craig follows through on a practice pass.

would have every opportunity to do so. But though he frequently performed nearly to perfection, he was always relegated to backup quarterback. Dallas was winning—up to a point—and Landry was not inclined to tamper with success.

In Craig's first season—the sixth season for Dallas —the Cowboys attained the .500 level at 7-7. The next season they were 10-3-1, winning the Eastern Conference championship. In the NFL title game the Cowboys were at the Green Bay goal-line trying for a tie when time ran out. They lost 34-27. The next season Dallas was only 9-5, but that was good enough for a pennant under the new four-division setup. The Cowboys routed Cleveland, 52-14, in the Eastern play-off. Once again Meredith was close on the Packers' heels before bowing, 21-17, to Green Bay in the league championship contest.

In 1968, Dallas took 12 games and lost two to win divisional honors again, but they were upset in the conference play-off by Cleveland. Meredith brooded all summer long about his inability to lead the team all the way. Shortly before preseason camp opened, he announced his retirement. Morton was fishing on the Russian River in Northern California when he heard the news on his portable radio. He was stunned.

"I simply couldn't believe it at first," he said. "Then I got excited. Here I had been given what I'd been waiting for. In a way, I would have preferred to earn it. As a friend, I was sorry to see Don go. As a team man, I was worried that it would weaken us. But as an individual I was sure I could step right in and get the job done."

Morton moved into camp with determination. He studied the play book to the point of exhaustion. He pasted plays on the walls so he could study them as he wandered about the room restlessly. He read them into a tape recorder so he could play it back to himself while falling asleep.

Morton, who had waited for so many years, was suddenly expected to go all the way to stardom in 1969. Rhome had been traded to Cleveland before Meredith's move. Roger Staubach, a former Heisman Trophy winner and Naval Academy All-America, had moved in, but he was deemed too rusty to pose a threat.

Staubach was 27 and had been in the service away from big-time football for six years. Still, he was such a spectacular scrambler that he made Morton keep moving. During his last two playing seasons at the Academy, he had averaged more than 60 percent in completions and more than nine yards a pass, while totaling more than 4,200 yards in total offense during his collegiate career.

Craig betrayed only traces of uncertainties. When the equipment manager asked him what number he wanted to wear in the first exhibition game, Morton smiled wistfully and said, "Number 17, preferably." That was Meredith's number, which had carried the Cowboys to considerable conquests. However, Mor-

ton remained with his number 14 and set out to make it known.

Despite near-crippling injuries, Craig succeeded so stunningly that he startled both his bosses and rivals. Coach Landry said, "When he stepped on the field, he was number one. I didn't think he'd be as demanding of other players as he was or take charge as quickly as he did or impress me as much as he did."

In an early workout, a coach criticized a player, who returned to the huddle, complaining. Morton grabbed him by the shoulder pads and said sharply, "I want to see you after practice." He later made it clear to the player that no one was above criticism.

Fine points separate one pro quarterback from another. Some are bigger, stronger, quicker, smarter than others, but those with the most size or most talent or most intelligence are not always the ones who do the best. The winners are those who combine all those qualities in just the right way, who do the best when it counts the most; and, sometimes, they are the ones who have the greatest support.

Morton had talented teammates, including a brilliant rookie running-back in Calvin Hill and remarkable receivers in Bob Hayes and Lance Rentzel. He used them wisely, calling most of his own signals in an offensive system matched in complexity

---

Morton gets the ball into the air a moment before he is knocked off his feet.

only by the one Len Dawson must operate in Kansas City.

He proved himself a superb passer to the sidelines as well as an exceptional deep thrower. Actually, strength is more important on sidelines passes than deep ones. With a few exceptions, most pros can loft a long one, but some do not have the power to whip the short ones through crowded areas to receivers who are guarded closely. Morton is so powerful he split Bob Hayes' fingers with some of his pegs.

"All around, I think I improved a lot," he says. "They talk about how long it takes to develop a pro quarterback, but I think I could have looked at movies and watched other players for ten years and not learned as much as I did in one year on the field, finding out things for myself. You find out what you can and can't do best only under fire.

"The pressure didn't bother me. Going in as relief for Meredith, I'd been under the gun in most of my infrequent appearances during my first four years as a pro. When you don't get many chances, you have to make the most of them, and that's as much a strain as being the big man."

As the big man took his team to a title, there were times, quite possibly because of injuries, when he did not do well. Fans, who loved the colorful Staubach, would chant, "We want Staubach." One time, Morton turned to Staubach and said, "Meredith used to hear them yelling, 'We want Morton,' sometimes. Your time will come."

Staubach smiled and said, "I know it will."

After the 1969 season ended, he submitted to a delicate operation in which ten inches of tendon were removed from a toe and foot and secured into his shoulder to replace a damaged ligament. The surgery was assessed as a success, though only the future will prove the point. After his three previous operations, Morton has become an old hand at hospitals.

"I don't like it, but I'm getting good at it," he says with a laugh. "I can tell when the nurses aren't following proper procedure now. I've been kind of cut up, so I have to wonder if what's left of me will hold up. But Bill Nelsen of Cleveland, who has nothing left to his knees, beat us in the play-offs, so where there's a will, maybe there's a way.

After his shoulder operation, Craig recuperates in the hospital.

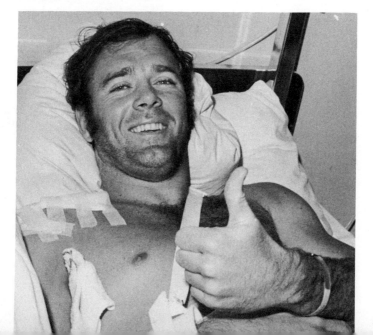

"Getting injured is an occupational hazard for quarterbacks. Most of us expect to be hurt all the time. We try to take it in stride and just hope it isn't too bad and doesn't curtail our careers. You need luck as well as ability and opportunity to succeed in this game. And my desire to play the game and succeed in it sees me through the rough times."

The 1969 loss to Cleveland was one too many play-off failures as far as the Dallas club is concerned. As the 1970s began, Landry admitted he was taking a long look at his approach and his personnel in an effort to figure out why they were falling short at the finish. In such situations, the quarterback is always spotlighted, and Morton admits that he himself has been depressed.

"I've thought about it ever since the game was over," he confessed. "I thought we were ready, more so than for any game in our history."

No one to alibi or evade blame, young Morton disregarded the critical injuries which curtailed his progress in what really was his rookie year as a regular—a spectacular one in spots. With better fortune physically and more experience may come consistency. This is all he needs to become a superstar and perhaps the leader of a championship team.

"It's a tough road to a championship game, a tough thing when everything comes down to one afternoon. But it's the way we have to go," he said. Morton is a young pro who has found out that the ultimate success can be elusive.

7
Bill Nelsen

In his third season as a professional, Bill Nelsen's right knee was wrenched so badly that he had to have one cartilage removed in an operation. The next season, his left knee was battered so badly that he had to have both cartilages removed in an operation. The following season, his right knee was smashed again.

"There is not much left to my knees," he admits with a sad sigh, "but I get by the best I can!" He practices in pain all week, then has fluid drained from the knees before playing with the Cleveland Browns on Sundays. During the 1968 and 1969 seasons, he led the Browns to Century Division pennants and Eastern Conference play-off crowns.

After the 1969 campaign, Nelsen resumed the extensive exercises which occupy his every off-season, working out with weights to strengthen his legs. "The stronger my legs are, the better chance my knees have," he explained. "All I can do beyond that is play the best I can and hope for the best. It

105

has not been easy for me to get here and I'd like to stay awhile if possible. Most people think my future is limited. But I've fooled a lot of people so far and I hope to go on fooling them."

William Keith Nelsen is another of those pro stars who took a roundabout route to the top. He might have dropped out of sports early from discouragement, but he stuck with it, maturing and developing late. Born January 29, 1941, on the east side of Los Angeles, Bill was interested in athletics at an early age. But at first he was too small to seriously consider a sports career.

"I never thought of becoming a pro or even a college star," he says. "I had enough to do just making my high school team."

Nelsen's early record as an athlete is tied in with his physical development. At 14, he stood 5 feet, 4 inches tall and weighed 115 pounds. A year later he had grown an inch and gained 20 pounds. The following year he had grown to a height of 5 feet, 10 inches and weighed 170 pounds. At 18, he was 5-feet-11 and weighed 180 pounds. Since then, he has added an inch and 15 pounds.

As a sophomore at El Rancho High School in nearby Pico Rivera, he was considered too small to play quarterback for the varsity, but big enough to play tackle for a reserve team. "That was the most fun I ever had," he says. "I got to hit people. However, I've been paid back in full since then."

BILL NELSEN

He began getting paid back when he became varsity quarterback as a junior. "I always tried out for quarterback," he recalls. "I couldn't run, but I could throw."

Still, he was a good enough athlete to star in basketball and baseball as well as football during his last two years in high school. The only college scholarship offer he received, however, was for basketball.

He preferred football, so he decided to attend junior college for a year with the hope of developing enough to interest a big school. This he did as star of Cerritos Junior College in Norwalk, California. He led Cerritos to a league title with an offense that averaged 46 points a game. The University of Southern California recruited him and he joined coach John McKay's Trojans.

After sitting out a season to permit further development, Nelsen became the team's regular quarterback. Bill passed for 446 yards that season. He passed for 683 yards as a junior and 682 yards as a senior, alternating with Pete Beathard both years.

Nelsen was not a polished performer during his college years. He threw for distance, not beauty, and moved awkwardly in the backfield. McKay preferred Beathard, who was a better runner and a more versatile performer in a college system.

Nelsen and Beathard did combine for more than 1,600 yards through the air as seniors. Nelsen was intercepted twice and Beathard just once as they set an NCAA team record with only three interceptions for the full season. They culminated the year with an exciting 42-37 victory over Wisconsin in the Rose Bowl.

Nelsen completed his college career with a modest statistical record, having completed less than half his passes, 104 of 238, for 15 touchdowns. Beathard was besieged with pro offers, though he spent the 1960s bouncing from team to team with an undistinguished record. While few pro teams were interested in Nelsen at first, he finished the 1960s as one of the game's dominant performers. He had not even been drafted after his junior year when his class graduated and he became eligible. He was drafted after his senior year only because one scout saw something in him others did not.

Fido Murphy, a colorful character who had studied college players for many pro teams over the years, called his selection of Nelsen, "The world's greatest upset." Fido was beating the bushes for Pittsburgh in those days, and the Steelers were startled when he recommended Nelsen to them.

"Beathard was a good college quarterback, but Nelsen had a pro arm," Murphy recalls. "A good all-around player may be a better college quarterback, but the passing specialist will be the better pro quarterback. Still, Nelsen was considered a second-stringer in college. The Steelers couldn't see him as a potential first-stringer in the pros.

"I had to trick them to take him. I told Buddy Parker, the coach, that Nelsen could make it as a defensive back, figuring once he got him, he'd find Nelsen could make it on offense, which is what happened. Nelsen couldn't play defense if his life depended on it, but the Steelers didn't know that. They took him on the tenth round when they had no one else to take, when nothing was left."

Coach Parker, who used to say, "A quarterback has to be around at least five years before he's anything as a pro," hardly looked at rookie Nelsen in 1962. But Bobby Layne had retired, so Nelsen hung on as third-stringer, throwing only two passes all season. The next year, Parker used Nelsen sparingly in only five games.

By 1965, Parker and Pittsburgh were in trouble. During an exhibition game in which Ed Brown and Tommy Wade were losing to Minnesota, 31-0, the coach turned to Nelsen and shrugged. "You might as well go in," he said.

Grabbing the opportunity, Bill threw for 175 yards and led the Steelers to three touchdowns in the final stages. He could no longer be ignored.

Parker, who had waited too long to turn to Nelsen, left Pittsburgh, and Mike Nixon took over as coach. Although Bill had injured his knee in the final exhibition contest, he played in twelve of fourteen regular-season games. Nelsen completed only 44 percent of his passes, but the Steelers were giving

Playing for the Steelers, Nelsen throws a pass against the Giants.

him scant support. The team won only two games. After the season, Nelsen had an operation to repair his knee.

Bill Austin became coach in 1966 and immediately confirmed Nelsen as his starter. The coach's confidence was rewarded when Bill led the team to 34 points and victory in the opener against the New York Giants. In their second game, however, Detroit's 300-pound Roger Brown landed on Nelsen's other knee, nearly destroying it. He had to submit to surgery again.

Once the cast was removed, Bill resolutely started to work out again so he could return for the final four games. He was absolutely brilliant. He completed 56 percent of his passes for more than 1,100 yards. At one point, he tied an NFL record by completing 13 consecutive passes.

In 1967, Nelsen reinjured a knee and required surgery again. He played in only eight games, completing only 44 percent of his passes. Pittsburgh won just four games. But the Cleveland Browns were impressed by Nelsen's flashes of brilliance despite his physical problems. They traded for him. With a good team and good luck physically, Nelsen developed rapidly.

Cleveland coach Blanton Collier turned to Nelsen after the Browns lost two of their first three games in 1968. Bill completed 16 of 25 passes for 190 yards in a 31-24 conquest of his former teammates, the Steelers. He was on his way. After playing creditably in a loss to St. Louis, Nelsen threw for three touchdowns in a 30-20 upset of Baltimore. Cleveland began rolling up a string of eight straight victories.

At the finish, the Browns had won 10 of 14 games and the Coastal Division crown. In the Eastern Division play-off against Dallas, the Cowboys were heavily favored, and they built an early lead. But Nelsen completed a 45-yard scoring pass to fullback Leroy Kelly to tie the contest, 10-10, at intermission.

Then, in the third quarter, the Browns were at midfield with third down and only inches to go. A running play was expected, but Nelsen faked a run to Kelly and threw a 20-yard strike to wide receiver Paul Warfield that broke the game wide open. The Browns went on to win, 31-20, and Nelsen received

Nelsen watches from the sidelines.

the greatest ovation of his checkered career from the 81,497 fans at Cleveland's Municipal Stadium.

Cleveland was outclassed by a booming Baltimore team in the NFL title game, 34-0, as the Colt defenders punctured Nelsen's protection and punished him badly. Despite the dismal windup, most observers felt that Bill Nelsen had established himself.

Veteran Cleveland player Jim Houston nicknamed him "Commander Nelsen," after Admiral Nelson, the British battle hero. Coach Collier said, "I've seen quarterbacks with great ability who cannot win. To win, you have to have confidence in yourself and in your teammates. Nelsen has it. He seeks advice and takes blame. Other players like that."

Nelsen said, "I've always known I wasn't a classic quarterback, but I always felt I was smart enough and strong enough to do the job if I could play with the proper help, which all came true in Cleveland. I just went out and took charge and did all the things I had been on the verge of doing for a long time. There were times I didn't do them, and as the quarterback and the key man, I accept the responsibility for failures such as we suffered in the title game."

In 1968, Nelsen completed 51 percent of his passes, for 2,366 yards and 19 touchdowns. In 1969, he improved in all categories—54 percent completions, 2,743 yards, 23 touchdowns. He carried Cleveland to a 10-3-1 record and another divisional crown.

Bill hands off to running back Leroy Kelly in the Browns' losing effort against the Vikings in the 1969 title game.

Post-season play in 1969 was almost identical to that of the previous season. Again the Browns were underdogs to the Cowboys and again they upset Dallas handily, this time before a howling enemy mob of nearly 70,000 persons in the Cotton Bowl. Nelsen took command early. He completed three passes on a drive to one touchdown, then three more to net another, then two more to a field goal that secured the issue. The Browns won in a breeze, 38-14.

Misfortune marked them in the NFL title game, however. Nelsen and his club came up short when a tackle by powerful defensive end Jim Marshall of the Minnesota Vikings mashed a nerve in Nelsen's throwing shoulder early in the game. Bill's arm went dead. He could throw, but without feeling. Meanwhile, the Cleveland defense collapsed and by the time Bill regained his touch, the Browns were down, 27-0.

Late in the game, Nelsen completed 18 yard passes to Milt Morin and Paul Warfield and a 3-yarder to Gary Collins, thereby salvaging seven points. Nelsen completed the game with respectable statistics, but he was depressed in the dressing room. "This can be a very discouraging game," he said. "Sometimes you can't win at all. Then you win and win and win and still fail to win at the finish."

But Bill Nelsen had been too close to the top to have any desire to quit the game. "It took me a long time to get to be a regular," he says, "and I expect to remain one now—until my knees give out or until my offensive line retires. I'll quit when it does."

A blithe spirit, Nelsen once took his blockers out to dinner to insure their grateful support in games to come. Maybe someday they will return the favor —perhaps by carrying Bill Nelsen off the field after he wins the championship for them.

8
Joe
Kapp

After eight years in Canadian football, Joe Kapp returned to the United States to play with the Minnesota Vikings. At the end of his third year back in the States, he and the Vikings were going for their first Western Division title against the powerful Los Angeles Rams. The Rams were heavily favored and ahead, 17-7, at halftime despite a 75-yard drive to a touchdown during which Joe Kapp had completed three critical passes to Gene Washington.

Joe sat in the Minnesota dressing room with his teammates and listened to coach Bud Grant, another Canadian convert, calmly conning them into thinking they still had a chance. Kapp really believed they could do it, too, because he is that way.

"I don't know what it is to quit and I wasn't about to quit then, with all that was at stake," he said in his harsh, hoarse voice. "I knew there was still time."

So old Joe Kapp, a big, tough veteran who runs awkwardly and throws awkwardly led his mates back out onto the field to outfight their foes before a crowd of 47,900 home fans who were screaming into the bitter cold. It was so cold the players' breath turned into steam and their hands and faces grew numb. But after all his years in Canada, Kapp was conditioned to cold—and to championships, too.

He began to move his club. He threw to flanker John Henderson at the sidelines, where Ram defender Jim Nettles was called for interference. Minnesota had reached its own 42. On the next play Kapp faded back, resisting the rush of Deacon Jones and Merlin Olsen and those other murderous Rams, and arched one of his wobbly passes far downfield. The ball was right on target—to end Gene Washington, who was tackled at the 11, then tackled again.

The second tackle, by Jack Pardee, cost the Rams a penalty to their 6. Kapp threw incomplete into the end zone. He went to throw again, but had no chance so he scrambled. He ran hard, vaulting players wherever necessary, till he reached the 1-yard line. Halfback Dave Osborn dove over for the score. With the extra point, Minnesota had closed the gap to 17-14. The Vikings went away whooping and hollering, full of spirit.

The Rams sagged as the Viking defensive line tore through the enemy's offensive line and Minnesota regained possession on its own 39. Osborn ran for 12. Bill Brown was thrown for a short loss, but Kapp threw one of his wobblers to Henderson for 24 yards to the Ram 27. Trying to pass, Kapp scrambled ferociously for 15 to the 12. Osborn gained one. Then Kapp passed and it was picked off by Ram defender Ed Meador on the four.

"That made me mad," Kapp said later.

The Viking defenders braced themselves and stopped the Rams again, forcing a punt to the Minnesota 34. Kapp called a run, then a long pass which missed, then a pass which Richie Petibon intercepted on the Minnesota 40. From there Roman Gabriel guided the Rams to a field goal that made the score 20-14 early in the final quarter.

"Now I was really seething," Kapp recalls.

He seemed to give off sparks as he spurred his spirited mates. Charlie West ran the kickoff back to the Minnesota 35. Brown ran for five, then Kapp threw to John Henderson for 20 yards to the Ram 40. Brown ran for nothing, but Kapp then rolled out and threw to Brown for 12. Brown ran for one and caught one from Kapp for eight. Osborn ran for three yards, then Kapp ran for 12. Osborn ran for two, then Kapp rolled around end for the last two, vaulting the last tackler. With the conversion, Minnesota suddenly led, 21-20.

The Rams were trapped deep after the kickoff and Gabriel, trying to throw from his goal-line, was hit by Carl Eller and dumped in the end zone for a

Kapp scores the winning touchdown against the Rams in the 1969 Playoff game. The Vikings won 23-20.

safety that made the score 23-20. Time was running short by the time the Rams got the ball back. Gabriel began to throw, but he was rushed hard and had trouble gaining much ground. He had reached the Minnesota 44 when his pass was picked off by Viking Alan Page. Kapp buried himself twice in the pit, the ball hugged to his belly. Then the gun went off, and Minnesota had its crown.

Afterward, in the joyous Viking dressing room, Grant and Kapp were talking about how tough the Rams were and what a great football player All-Pro quarterback Gabriel was, but all anyone else wanted to talk about was how tough Kapp was, and how tough he made Minnesota. "He may not be pretty, but he's pretty tough," one player said. Coach Grant said, "He gets knocked down, he never complains about a missed block or anything. He just gets up— he always gets up. They don't come much tougher."

Kapp himself said, "You gotta cut the rope out there. You can't hold anything back in this game, not if you're gonna be a man, and, more than a man, a part of this great thing we got going here on this team."

It took a long time for Joe Kapp to get that "great thing" going. Half-Mexican and half-German, he was born March 19, 1938, in Santa Fe, New Mexico. That is why he is sometimes called "Injun Joe," though he has no Indian blood in him—at least not American Indian blood. His father was a laborer and the Kapp family had nothing to spare. Joe grew up in a rough neighborhood. "It was important to be tough," he remembers.

He moved to Newhall, California, where he attended William S. Hart High School, named after the former cowboy movie star. Here he was an aggressive, but not a prominent football and basketball performer. He received only one major college scholarship offer—from the University of California at Berkeley—and that was to play basketball as well as football, which he did.

Kapp played fifth or sixth man on the basketball team; some said he played "hatchet man." He did well. At a height of 6 feet, 3 inches and weight of 210 pounds, he was a husky fellow to contend with on the court. Had he not reported late for practice every year (after the football season ended) he might have been a basketball star. But football came first.

Kapp didn't play much football during his sophomore year. He was sidelined with a knee injury. But he did come back late in the season to lead Cal to an upset of arch-rival Stanford, quarterbacked by All-America John Brodie. That was one of only three victories the Golden Bears scored in their ten games.

In 1957 Pete Elliott came in as coach and began rebuilding the team. With Kapp as regular quarterback, Cal won only one of ten games. But it was a different story in Joe's senior year. The Bears bounced all the way to the top of the Pacific Eight with seven victories in ten starts and a Rose Bowl appearance against Iowa, which they lost, 38-12.

Kapp is remembered on the California campus as an unpolished soul, a tough character who said little to anyone. He also was considered an unpolished performer on the field. During his college career, he completed 155 of 303 passes for 2,023 yards and eight touchdowns. He also rushed for 965 yards and returned kicks for 606 yards. He was considered as much of a runner as a passer, a rugged sort who was a better bet to make pro ball on defense than offense, but not a very good bet even at that. In the 1959 Hula Bowl All Star game, he was used as a defensive back, but he didn't like that.

When it came time for NFL choices, Washington drafted him, but not until the 12th round. (There was no AFL then.) The Redskins said that they might try him on defense, but actually they didn't bother to contact him at all.

Canadian Football League scouts, seeking "sleepers" who might be lured north of the border had Kapp on their list. Jim Finks, the boss of the Calgary team, contacted him and offered him a contract. Joe grabbed it.

"I didn't think I could make it in the NFL, though later found out I could," he admitted. "I wanted to play somewhere, not sit on the bench in the U.S. even if I made an NFL team. So I went, and I have no regrets."

He beat out Jack Kemp, who returned to the

United States and later became MVP in the AFL. Kapp played for Calgary two years, suffering knee problems, then was traded to Vancouver. In British Columbia, he was MVP in 1963 and led his team to the league championship in 1964. During eight years in Canada, he completed 1,476 of 2,709 passes for 22,725 yards and 137 touchdowns. This placed him second among that country's passers in the all-time records.

The Canadian league is a tough league, but Kapp is a tough man. Each team plays twice a week, on Saturday afternoon and Monday night. The field is longer and wider than fields in the United States. There is a twelfth man, so the quarterback has an extra receiver to whom to throw, as well as an extra defensive back to penetrate.

Most critically, he has three, not four downs on offense, so he must move the ball in two downs and gamble or turn it over on third down. When Kapp returned to U.S. football, he found that the extra down was like a "bonus." It seemed as if he had a lot more to work with.

He returned in 1967. Norm Van Brocklin had quit under pressure as coach at Minnesota but not until quarterback Fran Tarkenton had gotten his wish to be traded. Jim Finks had come from Canada to manage the team and, for coach, he had brought in Bud Grant, who had won five championships in Canada. They needed a quarterback and Finks recommended Kapp to Grant, who had faced him many times and respected him. Grant told Finks to go after him, and Kapp was lured away. "It was the challenge that excited me, plus a bit more money," Joe said.

Although Joe arrived with tremendous self-confidence, his first season wasn't anything to brag about. He completed less than half his passes for less than 1,400 yards and only eight touchdowns, and his team won only three of 14 games and finished last in the Central Division. Kapp got boos, not cheers.

The first time he faced the Rams, he lined up behind center, looked across the line at the "Fearsome Foursome" and said, "All right, you blankety-blanks, let's see how good you are." He found out.

The following year, 1968, Finks and Grant brought in Gary Cuozzo, a young veteran who posed a threat to Kapp's position. But Cuozzo suffered severe shoulder injuries and was sidelined. Meanwhile, Grant was rebuilding rapidly, developing a rugged defensive team. He needed only some offensive support to succeed. This he got, in part, from Kapp, who made adjustments to new demands. Joe completed 52 percent of his passes for nearly 1,700 yards and ten touchdowns. He ran 50 times for an average of five yards a carry, but he still struggled most of the way.

So did the team. Though Kapp had his days, com-

The rugged Viking quarterback takes the ball from center and another play begins.

pleting 16 of 20 passes for three touchdowns in a rout of Atlanta and two touchdown passes in a conquest of Washington, he seldom looked good. The boos resounded loudly whenever things went badly. In a critical game against Green Bay, Kapp completed only two of eleven attempts, but the Vikings struggled to a 10-7 triumph. Despite their problems the Vikings put together an 8-6 record, which was better than other teams in the Central Conference. So the Minnesota team had its first pennant.

In the Western Division play-off, Kapp really let go, completing 25 of 44 passes for both Viking touchdowns, but still the powerful Baltimore Colts ground out a 24-14 decision. Baltimore, however, went on to lose the Super Bowl in a stunning upset to the New York Jets, while Kapp and the Vikings began the long road back which, ironically, would lead them in 1969 to the same Super Bowl defeat that the Colts had experienced.

"I remember Vince Lombardi talking about the love that players on a good team feel for one another. We developed that love," tough old Joe Kapp says. "This was a darned good football team and we were bound to win."

Early in preseason play prior to the 1969 campaign, Kapp's knee folded under him and he was sidelined for a month. Gary Cuozzo took over and, after the Vikings had won five out of six exhibition games, was the starter for the regular-season opener. He lost that one, however, to the New York Giants, 24-23.

Grant turned to Kapp for the second game, against Baltimore. Joe fired the ball freely, completing 28 of 43 passes for 449 yards. In the process he tied an NFL record with seven touchdown passes. Afterward he growled, "It's a funny game . . ." Few could believe his performance against the defensive-minded Colts. Kapp convinced them, however, as the campaign wore on.

At times, he had troubles and was bailed out by Cuozzo, who relieved him to beat Green Bay and Pittsburgh. Kapp never complained. "He's a darned good quarterback. Any time I'm not doing the job, he can. We're a team," Kapp said. Grant liked Joe's spirit and teamwork.

Kapp remained the key regular, however. A week after Cleveland had destroyed Dallas, 42-10, the Vikings clobbered Cleveland, 51-3. Late in the season, Joe led a conquest of Gabriel and Los Angeles that ended an 11-game Ram winning streak and moved the Vikings to an 11-game streak of their own.

At the finish, Kapp had completed half his passes for 1,700 yards and 19 touchdowns. He ranked only tenth among NFL passers, but Minnesota had won the Central Division title at 12-2 and, after rallying to overcome the Rams in the Western play-offs, had only to beat Cleveland to rank first among NFL teams.

Acclaimed Viking MVP at a banquet, Kapp refused the honor, snorting, "There ain't no red-nosed reindeer. There ain't no Santa Claus. And there ain't no MVP on this team."

JOE KAPP

In the NFL title game against Cleveland, played in freezing weather before a sellout crowd of 47,900 in Minnesota, Kapp ran roughshod over Bill Nelsen and the Browns. He passed for one touchdown and ran for another. The latter was on a "broken play." As Kapp turned to hand off to Bill Brown, the two collided heavily. Kapp clutched the ball and barreled seven yards to score, hurdling a foe en route.

On the second play of the game, Kapp rocked the Browns by throwing deep to Washington and connecting on a 75-yard scoring thrust. From there the Vikings went on to a 27-7 romp.

Kapp, who had averaged 13 yards a pass and seven yards a run, trotted off to the cheers of the hysterical home crowd, then sat in the dressing room with blood dripping from his nose and said, "So I'm not a classic passer. Classics are for Greeks. I'm a winner."

In the Super Bowl, however, he was a loser. Lenny Dawson and the Kansas City Chiefs had upset Daryle Lamonica and the Oakland Raiders the week before in the AFL title game. Although they came into the game underrated, they were resourceful. The Vikings were reeling almost before they knew what had hit them. The Chiefs shot far in front.

In the second half, Kapp connected on five passes to drive his club 69 yards across the goal-line and

---

In the 1969 NFL Championship game, Kapp runs with the ball on a broken play and falls into the endzone for a touchdown. The Vikings beat the Browns 27-7.

133

back into contention. But soon after, end Aaron Brown, who had wrecked Lamonica the preceding week, rammed into the rugged Kapp with such force that the quarterback left the field in terrible pain, holding a damaged left arm. Being a right-hander, however, he stubbornly returned to battle. The Vikings lost, 23-7. Joe's only consolation was that he completed 16 of 25 passes for 183 yards, outpassing Dawson.

In the dressing room, a grimy Kapp growled. "So that's this year. So there's next year. We'll be back."

9
Daryle Lamonica

Quarterback of one of football's most successful teams, Lamonica shows his passing form.

Of all the "sleeper" draft choices who became star quarterbacks in pro football, none rates higher than Daryle Lamonica. The former Notre Dame signal caller was selected on the twelfth round by Green Bay of the NFL and the twenty-fourth round by Buffalo of the AFL. He went to Buffalo. He almost had his spirit broken during four years on the sidelines at Buffalo. Then he went to Oakland, where he led the Raiders to three divisional crowns, a league championship and the best record in football's major leagues over recent years.

This new-style, 6-foot, 3-inch, 215-pound quarterback can throw as hard as the strongest pitchers performing today. Although he takes more chances than most, he has had unusual success, capturing all but the ultimate crown. This, however, is not solely his responsibility, and sometimes it eludes the best of players.

"I know I rate with the best quarterbacks," he says. "I believe in Daryle Lamonica. I have no idol.

I have my own style. All I want is to be the best there is. I set my goals high."

Daryle Pat Lamonica was born on July 17, 1941, in Fresno, California, and reared in Clovis in the San Joaquin Valley. He was the only son of a rancher. The family owned 20 acres of fruit trees, and Daryle often picked peaches and apricots from sunup to sundown. At age six, he had a touch of polio and at thirteen he suffered through a siege of sleeping sickness. But he survived both and grew stronger. By the time he was in his teens, Daryle was an accomplished hunter and fisherman.

While he was in high school, his father appointed him foreman of their ranch to give him responsibility. Daryle worked hard, partly because of his love for the outdoors, but he also had time for high school athletics. He was a superb athlete who lettered in four sports. As a baseball player, he was an infielder with a home run swing. The Chicago Cubs offered him a $40,000 bonus to turn pro. "I wanted to jump at it," he recalls, "but my family and others preferred that I go to college. I could see the sense of that. Also, I wanted to play football."

As a teenager, Lamonica was big for his age so he played fullback for Clovis High School for two seasons. Then in his senior year, coach Lloyd Leest converted him to quarterback. Daryle performed exceptionally well in that spot and received many college scholarship offers. He accepted the one from glamorous Notre Dame.

138

Unfortunately, he arrived in South Bend at a time when the Fighting Irish were languishing under Joe Kuharich, the only coach in the school's history to compile a losing record. Kuharich used Lamonica sparingly, alternating him with Frank Budka and Ed Rutkowski, who have both since drifted out of sight.

However, life under the golden dome of Notre Dame still seemed glamorous to Daryle, who was moved by the sentiments of "Cheer, cheer for old Notre Dame." "Just to hear the fight song gets to you," he says. "Great spirit! It's in my blood and will be there until I die."

As it turned out, Lamonica was one of the least distinguished of many immortalized Notre Dame quarterbacks, though he went on to be a better pro than most of them. He received little national attention at a time when Terry Baker of Oregon State (the Heisman Trophy winner) and George Mira of Miami were the All-America quarterbacks.

Likewise, Daryle was given little chance of sticking in the big time after his last college game. Then he attracted notice with a spectacular performance in the East-West Shrine Game in Kezar Stadium, San Francisco, by completing 20 of 28 passes for 349 yards and driving his team 85 yards in the last two minutes to win. He earned unanimous Most Valuable Player laurels.

After the draft was held and the pro bidding began, he picked Buffalo over Green Bay. He figured he would have to wait a long time before replacing All-Pro quarterback Bart Starr of the Packers. As it turned out, he spent four years with the Bills without ever permanently displacing quarterback Jack Kemp. Kemp was a journeyman who came into his own in Buffalo. In fact, Kemp rose to all-star stature while Daryle was there.

Signed for a mere $2,000 bonus and $12,000 yearly salary, Lamonica played extensively only in his second season with Buffalo. That was a period when Kemp was having problems. Daryle bailed the Bills out, relieving in seven victories. The Bills won the Eastern Division title and beat out San Diego for the 1964 AFL title.

However, Buffalo coach Lou Saban kept going back to Kemp as his starter. He went almost all the way with Jack in 1965, when Buffalo repeated as divisional and league champion. Kemp was accorded MVP honors. Actually, Buffalo was a team oriented to defense and, while Kemp led the offense, he was completing only 45 percent or less of his passes in these years.

Still, Lamonica was no ball of fire at this time, either. His completion percentage declined steadily from 46 to 43 to 41 and finally to a dreadful 39 percent. He did concentrate on the "long bomb," however. He averaged almost 9 yards an attempt one season.

Shrewd Al Davis, the Oakland general manager, was impressed with Daryle. Davis, who used to go around saying, "If we could just get that big kid away from Buffalo . . .," finally did so in a daring deal in 1967. Davis traded his regular quarterback, Tom Flores, and All-Pro end, Art Powell, to the Bills for Lamonica and receiver Glenn Bass.

The trade ranks as one of the most one-sided in football history. While the others have fallen from the spotlight, Lamonica has risen to stardom.

Head coach John Rauch put Lamonica at the controls of the Raider offense right away. Daryle began to lead Oakland along the glory road with daring and determination.

"I'm grateful to Lou Saban," says Daryle of his Buffalo coach. "He didn't throw me to the wolves. He brought me along slowly. I developed during my four-year education in Buffalo. But I'm also grateful to Al Davis for having the faith to trade for me and to John Rauch for having the faith to use me. . . . I always had confidence in myself and always felt that all I needed was the opportunity to prove myself."

At first, Lamonica made a lot of mistakes in Oakland. He called the wrong plays or threw to the wrong places. At times in his first games he had his teammates bumping into one another. However, he didn't discourage easily, and he remained resourceful. He made "broken plays" work. Once he completely forgot the play he had called in the huddle. Instead of calling time at the line of scrimmage, he simply took the snap from center, kept the ball and ran around end for 18 yards.

Daryle impressed his teammates with his potential

for winning. Old pro George Blanda, his back-up quarterback, said, "He doesn't have as quick a release as Namath, but he has the strongest arm in football and he's more confident than any quarterback I've ever known." Lamonica used his arm to go for broke.

"I'm thinking of the end zone all the time," he explains. "I think there's less risk in passing once for fifteen yards than three times for five yards each. So my percentage is less than say, Len Dawson, who plays it cautious, who builds up his average with a lot of short completions. I get more yards and score more, which is what counts most."

No one argued with him. Halfback Pete Banaszak said, "He's the boss in the huddle. Try to talk and he tells you to shut up." Lamonica held himself apart from the others. "They call me a loner, because I don't believe in getting too close to other players," he says. "It's hard to chew out a friend and I may have to. I want respect, not popularity. Every receiver always thinks he's open. I decide where the openings are."

During his first season in Oakland, 1967, he completed 51 percent of his attempts, 220 of 425, for 3,228 yards and a league-leading 30 touchdowns. The Raiders won a league-record 13 out of 14 games and breezed to the Western Division pennant. La-

---

Lamonica talks to a teammate on the sidelines.

monica was named Most Valuable Player, completing a dramatic rise to prominence.

In the key game in December against San Diego, he completed 21 of 34 passes for 323 yards and four touchdowns, resulting in a 41-21 romp. In the AFL title game, he passed the Raiders to an easy 40-7 rout of Eastern Division survivor Houston. On one play, Daryle passed for a touchdown after faking a field goal.

The victory over Houston put Daryle and his mates in the second Super Bowl contest, played in the Orange Bowl in Miami—against mighty Green Bay. The Raiders were simply outclassed by their NFL rivals. Two field goals and a Bart Starr-to-Boyd Dowler pass play of 62 yards brought Green Bay to a 13-0 advantage. Lamonica, playing boldly in an effort to overcome the odds, drove his team 55 yards, then passed to flanker Bill Miller for 23 yards and a touchdown. However, a teammate later fumbled a kick, setting up another Green Bay score and a 16-7 lead at the intermission.

In the second half, the Packers drove through the Raider defense for a field goal and a touchdown, and cornerback Herb Adderley picked off a Lamonica pass, returning it 60 yards for one more touchdown. Although Daryle reached Miller for another 23-yard score, it mattered little. The final count was 33-14, in favor of Green Bay.

Lamonica, who had completed 15 of 34 passes for 186 yards, shrugged off the defeat. "We made mistakes," he said, "but they were aggressive mistakes. We carried the fight to them more than Lenny Dawson and Kansas City did last season in the first Super Bowl. We lost the game. But we came out a winner, convinced we could beat anybody."

In 1968, Lamonica came back with 206 completions in 416 attempts, a shade below 50 percent, for 3,245 yards, 25 touchdowns. On the last day of the regular season, Lamonica brought his team from behind in the second half to a 34-27 victory in San Diego, connecting on touchdown passes of 13, 40 and 55 yards. That put the Raiders in a divisional play-off with Kansas City. Lamonica erupted with five touchdown passes against the Chiefs while rival quarterback Len Dawson was intercepted four times. The Raiders won, 41-6.

The AFL championship game was played before a record crowd of 62,627 fans in Shea Stadium, New York. The Raiders had beaten the Eastern title-winning Jets twice during the season and were favored. But Joe Namath took New York to a 10-0 lead early in the game. Lamonica brought the Raiders back into the contest with a drive that culminated in a 29-yard scoring pass to Fred Biletnikoff. The two teams swapped field goals before halftime, leaving the Jets in front, 13-10, at intermission.

It was a cold, gray day, and the noise of the fans beat down on the weary players. In the third quarter, Lamonica drove the Raiders deep into Jet terri-

tory, where George Blanda booted a three-pointer to tie the score. But Namath connected with a 20-yard scoring pass to Pete Lammons to put the Jets in front again.

In the final quarter, with 12 minutes to go, Lamonica led the Raiders 57 yards to the Jet 11. A run failed on first down. He overthrew a receiver on second down. A pass to Billy Cannon was batted down on third down. Blanda kicked a field goal on fourth down to narrow the count to 20-16.

When the Jets took over, Namath was intercepted on his own 37. Lamonica then led the Raiders to a touchdown that put the Raiders ahead, 23-20. Namath came right back with a drive that finished with a 6-yard scoring pass to Maynard, making the score 27-23, for the Jets.

After the kickoff, Oakland took over on its own 34. Though the California team got the ball rolling, they couldn't score.

The Raiders got the ball back again on their own 15 with 3:27 to play. Determinedly, Lamonica drove down the field. He hit Biletnikoff for 24 yards, then Warren Wells for 37. The Jets were penalized back to their own 24. With two minutes left, Oakland was on the verge of pulling it out.

Lamonica went for a swing pass to Charlie Smith, throwing wide to the receiver who was supposed to move behind a screen of blockers. Daryle didn't

---

Daryle fakes a hand-off to a running back.

drop back far enough and Smith didn't run forward enough. The pass went behind Smith and fell incomplete. However, the ball had been thrown laterally, and was considered a lateral. As such it was a free ball, which few realized in those moments. Smith himself did not realize it while the ball lay at his feet. A Jet grabbed it and the game was all over.

The Jets went on to upset Baltimore in that momentous Super Bowl triumph for the AFL. Afterward, a wistful Lamonica observed, "It could have been us. We should have beaten the Jets in the play-off. And if we had, we'd have beaten the Colts in the Super Bowl just as they did. I'm sure of it." Coach Rauch called to console Daryle. Lamonica said, "Don't worry, coach, we'll get them next year."

The Raiders came back in 1969 to another superb season, 12-1-1, and a third straight Western Division title. Lamonica completed 221 of 426 passes, almost 52 percent, for 3,302 yards and 34 touchdowns. In the first exhibition game, Daryle jammed his hand and thumb on an opponent's helmet so he had to play the first two weeks of the regular season with a cast on his throwing hand. He did poorly and was booed.

But he came back against Buffalo to throw six touchdown passes in the first half alone. He narrowly missed a seventh when the receiver was forced out at the 6-yard line.

After that, he pulled a hamstring muscle in one leg, stretched ligaments in his left knee, tore muscles in his left shoulder and suffered back and rib injuries. In Miami, where the heat was excessive, he suffered from cramps, but he kept going.

The day before the San Diego game, Lamonica was hospitalized with a severe case of the flu. He could not stop vomiting, lost 10 pounds and had a fever of 103 degrees. On the morning of the game, he asked to be released to play. A thermometer was placed in his mouth. He held it with his teeth, careful not to let his tongue touch it. Because the thermometer showed no excessive temperature, he was released. He played—completing 19 out of 26 passes, three for touchdowns. The Raiders won.

The next week, still weak, he was intercepted five times as the Cincinnati Bengals and Greg Cook handed the Raiders their only loss of the season, 31-17. Before the next game, against the Jets, Lamonica suffered back spasms, but pitched a victory. The next week he was hospitalized with the same problem. On Sunday he came out to throw three touchdown passes for a revenge victory over Cincinnati. Despite his physical problems during the regular season, it was quite a year.

The AFL had gone into a two-part play-off system in 1969. The champion of one division met the runner-up in the other division, and the survivors met for the title. In the first phase of the play-off, the Raiders met Houston on a slippery field in Oakland. Lamonica threw a wet ball for 13 completions in 17 attempts, 276 yards, and six touchdowns. The Western champion, Oakland, crushed the Eastern runner-up, Houston, 56-7. Meanwhile, the Western runner-up, Kansas City, upset the Eastern champion, New York.

Lamonica and Oakland had beaten Dawson and Kansas City twice during the regular season. In addition, Oakland had posted the finest one-season record in AFL history. Thus, the Raiders were heavily favored to win against a runner-up team that would have been eliminated under the old rules.

But when the showdown came, the Kansas City defensive line overpowered the Oakland offensive line. Yet while the Chiefs kept punishing him, Daryle carried the Raiders to an early lead. Then in the third quarter, defensive Kansas City end Aaron Brown, who had already thrown Lamonica for losses three times, barged into him just as he passed. Lamonica's hand was jammed on Brown's helmet.

Lamonica went to the sidelines, shaking his hand in despair. He missed thirteen plays before he returned. "I had no feel for the ball," he admitted later. His passes mostly missed or were picked off. The Raiders lost.

Weary and woeful, Lamonica hung his head in the dressing room. His "dead" hand hung limply at his side. "We could have won," he kept saying over and over again.

Kansas City went on to upset the Minnesota Vikings, giving the AFL its second straight Super Bowl success. "It should have been us," Lamonica sighed.

DARYLE LAMONICA

After seven seasons as a professional, Lamonica had thrown for more than 12,000 yards and 105 touchdowns. After three seasons as a Raider, he had led his team to three divisional crowns, a league title

In the 1969 AFL championship game, Lamonica is grabbed from behind by Kansas City lineman Buck Buchanan after a pass has been thrown.

and a combined record of 37-4-1, unsurpassed for any three-year period in professional football history.

The newly found success meant newly found critics for Daryle. One lady columnist said the football bachelor was one of the ten most conceited players. "She mistakes confidence for conceit," retorted Daryle. "I think that what counts is how you live and how you conduct your life."

Lamonica conducts his life in a grand way. But it is his way, and it is pretty much a quiet way. For example, in the long-hair era, Daryle is somewhat of an individualist with his short hair. "I don't pop off and I don't go for mod clothes," he says. "I guess I'm not very colorful."

He prefers big-game hunting around the world to hunting for publicity in Hollywood or New York.

"I love the outdoors life," he says. "I think the best time of the day is between daybreak and sunrise, when the birds and flowers are coming alive. There is nothing like it."

If Lamonica's opponents harbor any thoughts that he may trade in his football jersey for a hunting jacket, they should listen further. "Football still excites me, though," he adds. "It is part of me. If I can only win the championship with my team, I could not ask for much more. I think I can."

10
Lenny
Dawson

The first Super Bowl game was played on a sunny Sunday before more than 60,000 fans in the cavernous Coliseum in Los Angeles at the conclusion of the 1966 season. The mighty Green Bay Packers, the champions of the National Football League, were heavily favored to defeat the Kansas City Chiefs, kings of the upstart American Football League. But the Chiefs were keeping the game close.

Bart Starr collaborated with Boyd Dowler on a long scoring pass that put the Packers on top, 7-0, and most of the spectators settled back to wait for the rout to begin. However, Lenny Dawson drove the Chiefs right back, connecting on passes of 17 yards to Mike Garrett, 41 yards to Otis Taylor and seven yards to Curtis McClinton for the tying touchdown.

Green Bay marched 73 yards to move back in front, 14-7, but Dawson guided the Chiefs into field-goal range to cut the count to 14-10 at halftime.

Early in the second half, Kansas City was carrying

155

the fight to the favored foe, and on third down near midfield Dawson called for a pass to Fred Arbanas. Dawson was surprised as the Packers blitzed and rushed his throw, which linebacker Dave Robinson deflected to safety Willie Wood. It was a freak play that finished on the Kansas City 5-yard line. It also finished the Chiefs. After Elijah Pitts rammed home a score, the Packers rolled to a 35-10 triumph.

In the tomb-like Kansas City dressing room after the game, a pale Lenny Dawson said, "It's been a long, hard way to here, but we'll be back no matter how long it takes and how hard it is."

Probably, it took longer and was harder than he anticipated. But nothing ever came easy to Lenny Dawson.

Leonard Ray Dawson was born June 20, 1935, in Alliance, Ohio. He was one of seven brothers, and altogether there were eleven children in the family. Their father was a machinist who worked in a mill to eke out a difficult living for his large family in the small, tough industrial town. The Dawsons had no money for luxuries.

The boys played ball on the sandlots. "I remember getting up and going out at eight in the morning and playing all day," Len said. "When I was young, I was small, so I took a beating. But my brothers all played and I had to play, too."

In such a large family, he was almost overlooked. Once when he was eleven years old, Lenny and the rest of his family went to a baseball game in Cleveland. When it was over, Lenny stopped in the rest room. The family piled into its two old station wagons and took off without him, never missing him. Lenny wandered around for a while, finding another lad who was lost and weeping in the deserted stadium. Lenny called home collect, and his parents wired enough money for him to take the bus home.

He was always a calm, calculating boy. A good all-around athlete, he lacked size. He played basketball and baseball in high school, hit .400 in American Legion ball, and preferred baseball to football because he only weighed 125 pounds at age fourteen. He admits that he never cared for the violence of football. He didn't enjoy getting hit.

He went out for the high school team only because his brothers had all played football and it was expected of him. As a sophomore, he played fifth string. By the time he became a junior, Alliance's number one quarterback had a dislocated shoulder, and the others had graduated. Lenny was given a starting assignment because no one else had worked at the position.

He remembers facing a heralded Steubenville High lineman named Cal Jones, who went on to Iowa and professional stardom. "He looked enormous to me. You talk about fear, I had it," Lenny said. "That's when I developed my quick release."

He did have a quick release and a good arm. He grew to be 6 feet tall, though he weighed only 170 pounds. He had a good junior year and an outstanding senior year, winning All-State honors.

He wanted to go to college and several schools offered him athletic scholarships. Ohio State was interested in him, but they did not pass much and ran out of a split-T formation. "I couldn't see myself running down the line and getting my head torn off," said Lenny. When they tried to tell him that it was practically his patriotic duty to go to his home-state college, he became totally disenchanted and decided, instead, to accept an offer from Purdue, which was also interested in him as a basketball player.

At Purdue, Dawson shook up some of his superiors with his reserved cynicism. When basketball coach Ray Eddy said, "I know you'll be a big help to us in basketball," Dawson looked him in the eye and replied, "You don't know that; you've never seen me play." Actually Lenny proved to be more help to them in football. Before his first game, an assistant coach said, "I want to wish you luck." Len said, "You don't need luck, only ability." He demonstrated his ability though later on, as a pro, he found he needed luck, too.

In his first game, he completed 11 of 17 passes for 185 yards and four touchdowns in a 31-0 rout of Missouri. In another early game, he threw four more touchdown passes to upset Notre Dame, 27-14. He went on to lead the Big Ten in passing for three straight seasons and completed his college career with 243 completions in 452 attempts for 3,325 yards. He was also honored as an All-America.

Dawson was selected on the first round of the college draft by the NFL's Pittsburgh Steelers. However, he was not used in the All-Star game since Paul Hornung and John Brodie played quarterback. Nor was he used in Pittsburgh, for coach Buddy Parker had Bobby Layne to play quarterback. Later, even Ted Marchibroda and Jack Scarbath ranked ahead of him.

It is incredible how seldom Lenny played. He got to throw four passes during his first season, six his second and seven his third. Pittsburgh had fair teams in those years, but it did not give Dawson a fair chance. Parker felt Lenny lacked leadership qualities, though it is hard to understand how he decided this. Dawson never had the chance to lead the team.

Coach Paul Brown needed a spare quarterback in Cleveland. He recalled Dawson's collegiate credentials and figured he was an experienced pro now after three seasons in the NFL. So Brown made a minor deal for him in 1960. However, Milt Plum was his regular and full-time player, and Brown decided that Dawson was too small and didn't have a strong enough arm to be much more than an emergency backup man. That season Dawson threw thirteen passes and during the next season he threw fifteen. After five years, he had gotten to pass 45 times, less than some quarterbacks do in one game.

After the 1961 season, Dawson was deeply discouraged. "I didn't demand a chance in Pittsburgh and Cleveland, so perhaps part of not playing was my fault," he said. "But I worked hard and waited for an opportunity which never came. I finally began to feel that, if two top coaches had observed me a little and were not interested in using me, maybe I wasn't really good enough. Maybe I was wasting my time and should quit."

Fortunately for Dawson, he encountered Hank Stram, who had been an assistant coach when Len was at Purdue and was now the head coach of the Dallas Texans of the American League. Stram remembered Dawson as a skillful passer, potentially superior to most in the new curcuit. He reasoned that if Dawson had anything left after five wasted seasons, he could help the Texans.

He told Lenny, "If you leave Cleveland and want a job, give me a call." Dawson hesitated because he was on the verge of retiring. After thinking it over, he went to Brown, who was about to cut him anyway. Dawson asked for his release and Brown gave it to him. Dawson called Stram, and they arranged for him to join the team for the 1962 season.

Dawson really did not have a strong arm, but he handled the ball beautifully and he threw a wide variety of passes, mostly short ones, with deadly accuracy. He also was a cool, calculating player and a shrewd strategist.

160

When he reported to his new camp, he was rusty and out of shape. For a while he tripped over his own feet. "I was terrible," he recalled. "If my coach had been anyone but Stram, who knew me from the past, I'm sure he'd have cut me."

Stram said, "I was shocked at how bad he was at first, but I couldn't help but realize that five years of sitting on a bench or manning telephones didn't make a man sharp. I stuck with him and he swiftly smoothed out the rough spots."

Stram's teams employ the most complex offenses in football, outside of those used by Tom Landry's teams, but they have one advantage for a quarterback. They place him in a "moving pocket." As he rolls out, his blockers roll with him. The tacklers never know which way he is going to go and must always penetrate protection to get at him. Dawson had to learn a lot of plays to master his new team's tactics, but he got the sort of help he needed.

Once given the opportunity to play first-string, Dawson was an immediate sensation. During his first year he completed an astounding league record of 61 percent of his passes, 189 of 310, for 2,750 yards and a league-leading 29 touchdown passes and average per pass of almost nine yards. He led the team to eleven victories in fourteen games and the championship of the AFL's Western Division. He was also selected to the All-Star team and named Most Valuable Player.

The AFL title game turned out to be the longest

in football history. Dawson led the team to a 17-0 halftime lead. However, Houston, the Eastern champion, rallied behind George Blanda to tie the score at the end of regulation time. After a scoreless first overtime period, the two teams went into a second overtime session. Finally, 77 minutes and 54 seconds after the game had begun, Texas rookie Tommy Brooker kicked a 25-yard field goal to settle the championship contest, 20-17.

Dawson and his mates ran off in triumph. "After what I had gone through, it had to be the greatest thrill of my life," Dawson recalls. "It was like being reborn."

Although that was his sixth year as a pro, it really was his rookie year as a regular. AFL critics used Dawson as an example of the glaring mediocrity of the new circuit, contending that if a castoff cut by the old league after five years of being found inadequate could become the league's new star and lead a team to a title in his first try, then the league could not be much.

In time, however, Dawson would disprove this reasoning. He simply had not been given a chance in the old league. Given a chance in the new league, he demonstrated excellence.

During eight seasons in the AFL, through the end of the 1960s, Lenny consistently completed 56 percent or more of his passes for long yardage. By the

---

Lenny shows intense concentration as he fires a pass.

end of this time, he had completed more than 1,300 passes for more than 18,000 yards and 182 touchdowns. He never had as many as 20 passes intercepted in a season, and he averaged close to nine yards an attempt during several seasons. In pro football history, only Bart Starr and Sammy Baugh had higher completion percentages; only Otto Graham and Norm Van Brocklin averaged more yards per pass.

"He may be the most accurate passer football has known," says Stram. "Although he doesn't throw deep as much as most quarterbacks, or, for that matter, as often as most, he picks his spots and is deadly with those he does throw, gaining enormously with them. He is a very smart fellow and a gifted all-round performer. He is not a holler-guy and I've never seen him show great emotion, but he is smart and firm, has gained his teammates' respect and leads by example. He is capable of great highs and seldom has excessive lows."

Dawson led the league in passing four times, in touchdown passes four times (he did not lead in 1964 when he reached his personal high of 30) and twice was selected the All-Star quarterback. He was the outstanding offensive player in the annual All-Star game following the 1968 season. He has statistics which few players can match, despite his having wasted five seasons.

In Dawson's second season in the AFL, his team shifted from Dallas to Kansas City, where they were

nicknamed the Chiefs. The move may have unset-
tled them but, more important, some of the team's
early stars were wearing out and Dawson had to operate with modest support. The Chiefs dropped to a
5-7-2 record and rose only slightly to 7-7 the following season and to 7-5-2 the next campaign. But
by 1966 Stram had rebuilt them to excellence with
an 11-2-1 record and a divisional title.

Dawson tackled Buffalo in the 1966 title play-off
in front of 42,080 frozen fans in the upstate New
York city. Three plays after the opening kickoff,
Dawson threw 29 yards to Arbanas for the first
touchdown. A little later, he threw 29 yards to
Taylor for another touchdown. Later, he threw 45
yards to Chris Burford to set up another score. In
all, Dawson completed 16 of 24 tries for 227 yards
and a 31-7 romp to victory.

Then came the Super Bowl and a crushing disappointment when Green Bay defeated the Chiefs.
Lenny and his fellow players had to begin the long,
hard road back.

In 1967, they were 9-5 and second to Oakland in
the West. In 1968, they were 12-2 and tied for first
with Oakland in the West, but finished second again
when Oakland rolled up a crushing 41-6 victory as
the Chiefs collapsed in the deciding game.

In 1969, Kansas City twice lost to Oakland during
the regular season and finished at 11-3, second again
to Oakland in the West. This time, however, there
was a difference. In its final year before fully merg-

ing with the NFL, the AFL had instituted the two-part play-off in which the champs of each division would play the runners-up of the other division with the survivors meeting for the title. If Kansas City could conquer Eastern champion New York, they could get another chance at Oakland for the league title and a place in the Super Bowl.

Early in the 1969 season, Lenny Dawson had suffered torn ligaments in his left knee in a game against Boston. The team doctor wanted to operate immediately. Dawson asked to see a consulting specialist. Dr. Fred Reynolds of St. Louis was called in and said he felt that, if Dawson rested, the tears possibly would heal by themselves without surgery. Lenny might be able to play in five or six weeks.

"I had suffered more painful, if not more serious injuries," Dawson recalls. "I'd played with broken ribs and jammed hands. I wasn't 24. If I had been, I'd probably have had the operation. But I was 34 and I knew I wouldn't be playing much longer. We had a chance for a championship if I would play this season. If I had an operation and didn't play and we lost, well there might not be much future for an old bum-legged quarterback. I decided to wait and hope for the best."

While he waited, Mike Livingston took over.

Dawson is in trouble with Oakland tacklers. The Chiefs lost the AFL championship to Oakland in 1967 and 1968, but won it in 1969.

167

After five weeks, Dawson returned, hobbled by a brace on his knee. Despite his physical handicaps, Dawson finished the season respectably, completing 59 percent of his passes for more than 1,300 yards, and Kansas City remained alive. In the first play-off game, Dawson pitched the Chiefs past Joe Namath and the New York Jets in New York, thus setting up the rematch with Oakland.

This time Dawson and the Chiefs were ready. Oakland led early in the game, but Dawson connected on a long pass to Frank Pitts (42 yards) to the Raider 1-yard line to set up the tying score before halftime. In the second half, Oakland's Lamonica jammed his hand on Aaron Brown's helmet and after that he was ineffective. The final score was 17-7. The Chiefs were the champions of their league, headed for another Super Bowl game.

Then a storm broke. Dawson was named as one of several athletes who had received telephone calls from a bookmaker involved in a gambling probe. On such a flimsy circumstance, Dawson had been publicly implicated in a scandal on the week of his greatest game. Quietly protesting his total innocence, Dawson seemed bewildered as he practiced in preparation for the spectacular against Minnesota in the Sugar Bowl in New Orleans. Though he tried not to think about the scandal, it was part of his life. He had trouble sleeping.

On the day of the big game, there were 80,997 persons in the Sugar Bowl, with millions more watching on television. As calm as though nothing could bother him, Dawson mounted drives to three field goals and suddenly the Chiefs were in front of the heavily favored Vikings, 9-0. Minnesota began to come unglued. A fumbled kickoff set up the Chiefs for another score, a touchdown by Mike Garrett. Now the score was 16-0.

Most had considered the Jets' upset of the Colts the year before a fluke, just one of those things that can happen in a game. It scarcely proved that the AFL had risen to equality with the NFL. Now they wondered. As Joe Kapp jarred the Chiefs with a second-half touchdown drive that reduced the deficit to 16-7, most of the onlookers expected Kansas City to collapse.

Instead, with third and six on his own 32-yard line, Dawson cleverly faked a pass and handed off to Otis Taylor for an end-around run that produced seven yards and a first down. Reaching the Minnesota 46, Dawson called a pass to Lionel Taylor, pitched perfectly to him. Taylor broke tackles en route to the end zone. It was the touchdown that broke the game wide open.

Kansas City won, 23-7, establishing AFL equality. Dawson, who had completed 12 of 17 passes for 142 yards, who had called 18 different formations in one string of 18 plays, was informed in the riotous dressing room that he had won the sports car presented by *Sport* magazine to the Most Valuable Player of pro football's championship game.

LENNY DAWSON

Suddenly, Lenny Dawson was king of kings. He sat, thin and weary and soiled, gently rubbing his sore knee. Someone asked him what he thought of his performance. "Well, we won," he said. His son stood by his side, touching his father with one hand. Someone asked the boy what he thought. "He's the greatest," the lad said softly.

Then Lenny was called to the telephone. President Richard Nixon was calling from Washington to congratulate him.

The ordeal was over—the ordeal of all the years up to this time, including the seasons when no one would play him; the ordeal of this particular year, when his knee was so badly injured and he risked playing on it without an operation, and the ordeal of his senseless implication in a scandal.

"No one will ever know what I've gone through inside," he admitted quietly. He smiled a little, the dirt and sweat of battle marking his thin body, and said, "I've had my ups and downs. I guess a lot of players do. Now I'm at the top of the heap. Some great ones never get there. It's hard to believe," he said.

After winning the 1969 Super Bowl for the Chiefs, Len receives telephone congratulations from President Nixon.

Index

Page numbers in italics refer to photographs

INDEX

173

INDEX

INDEX

176

About the Author

Bill Libby is a free lance sportswriter who lives in Los Angeles. He is the author of a recent book on Parnelli Jones and is a frequent contributor to *Sport* Magazine.